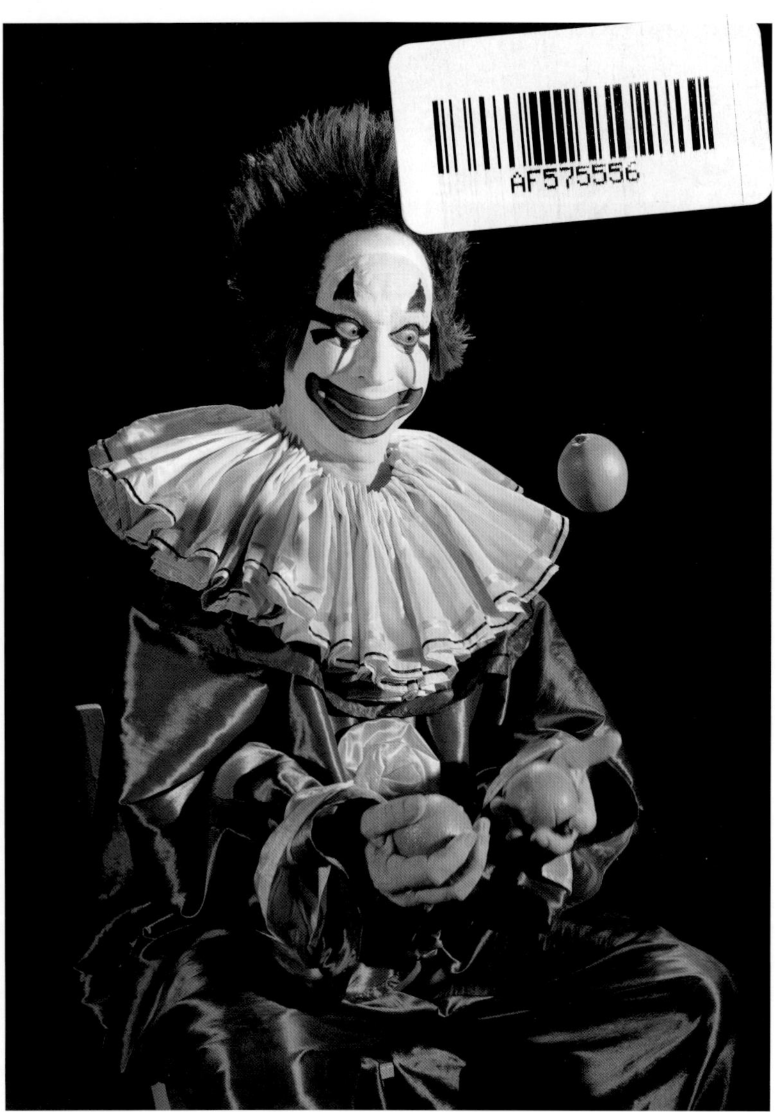

Clown, 1946, 2010

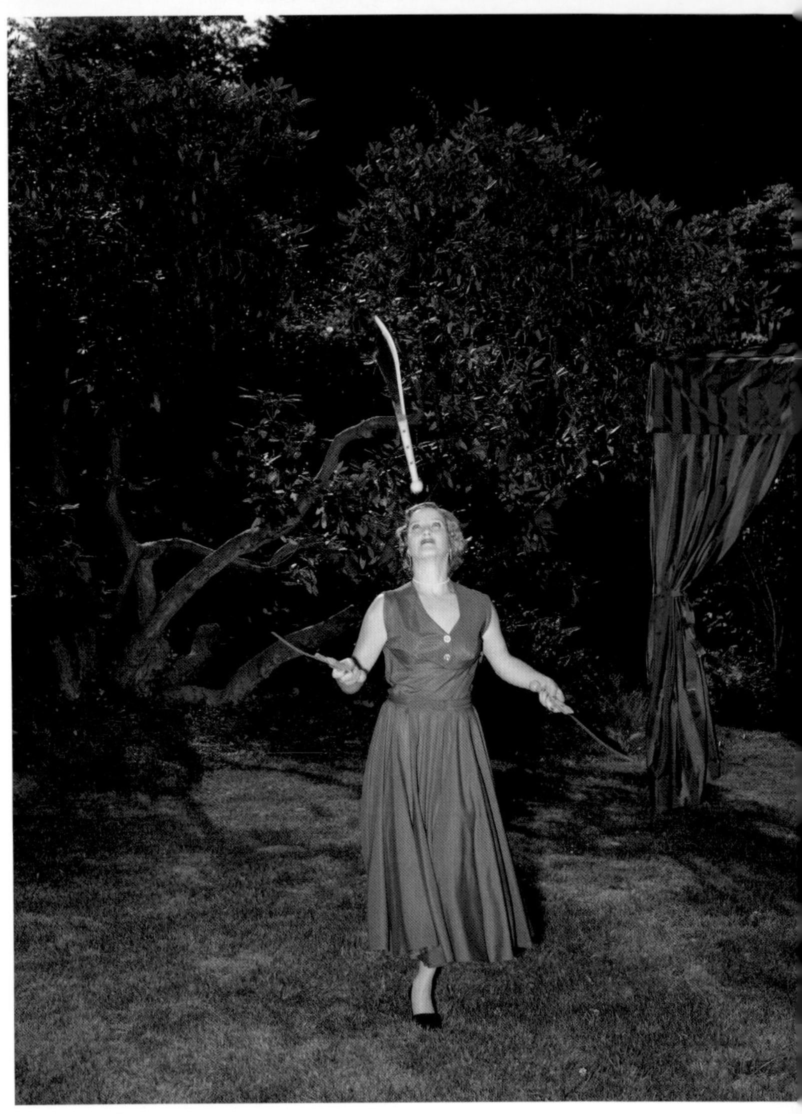

Juggler, 1946, 2010

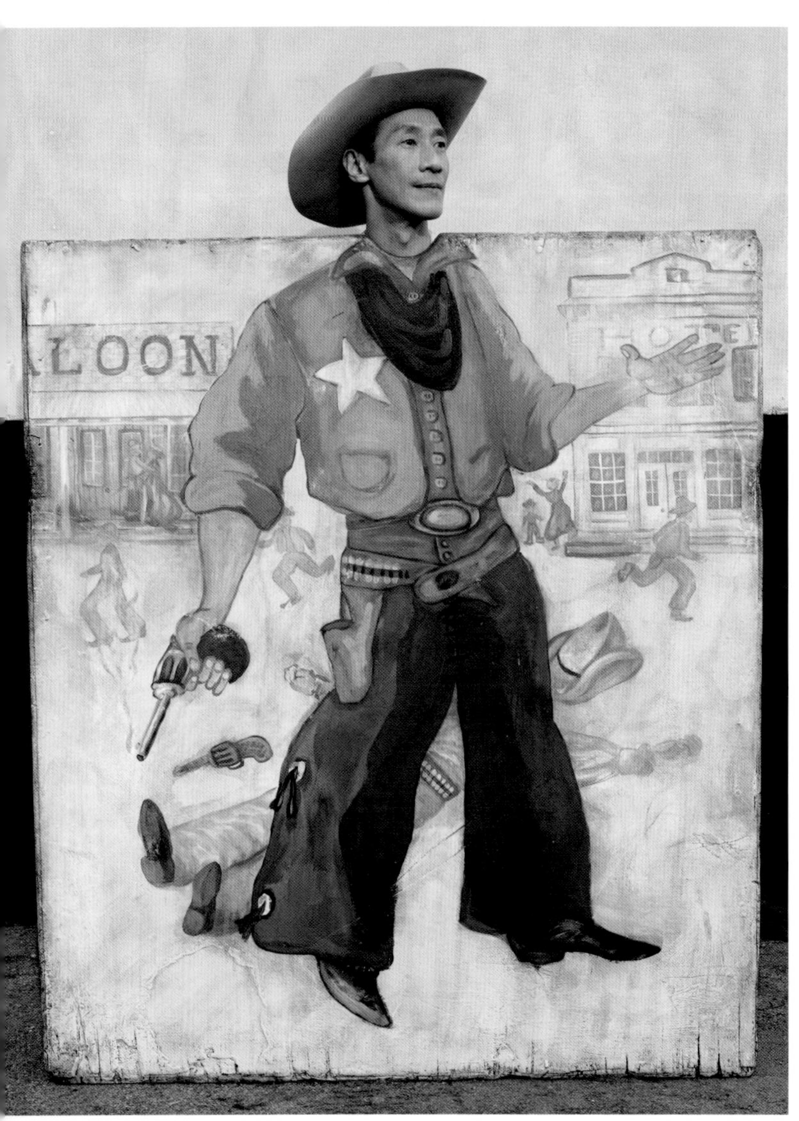

Passe-tête, 1946, 2010

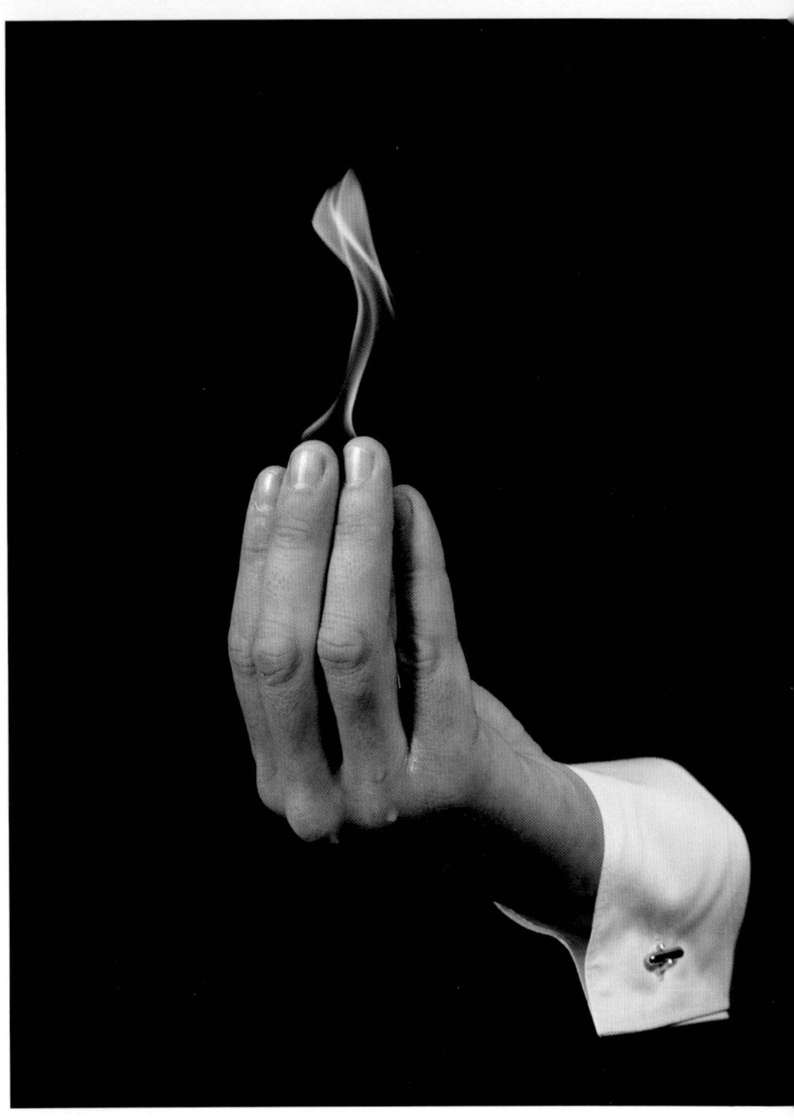

Flame, 1947, 2010

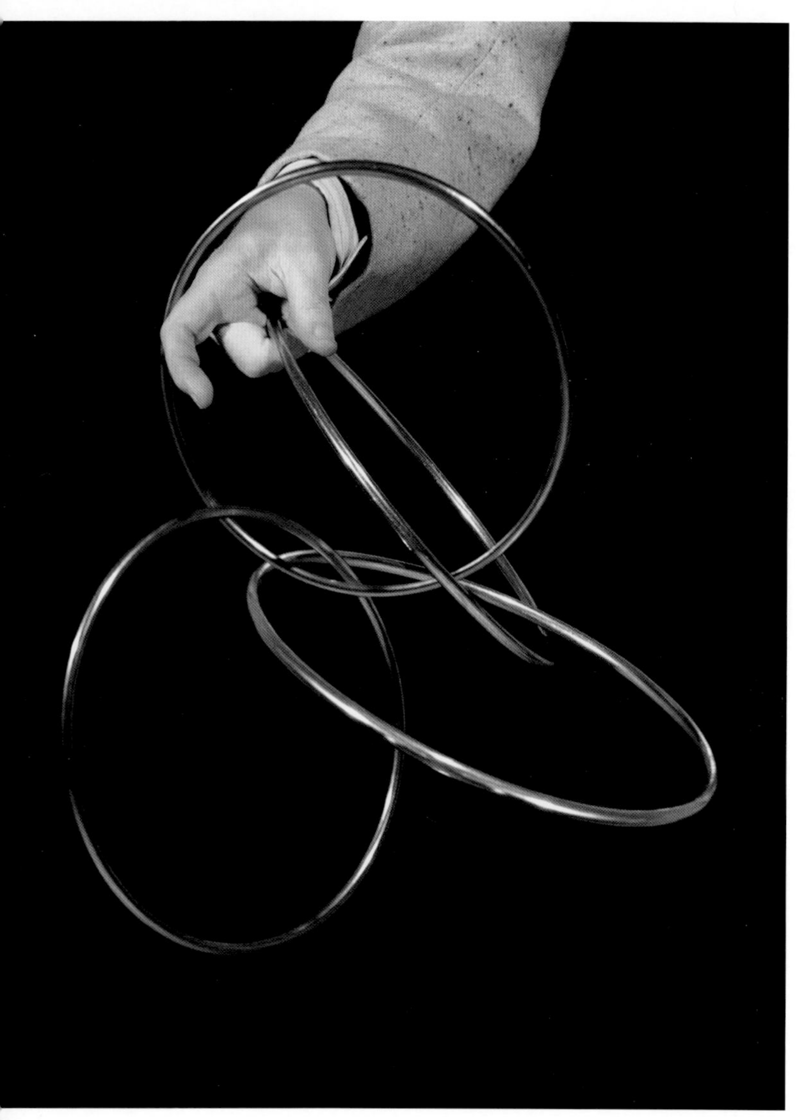

Rings, 1947, 2010

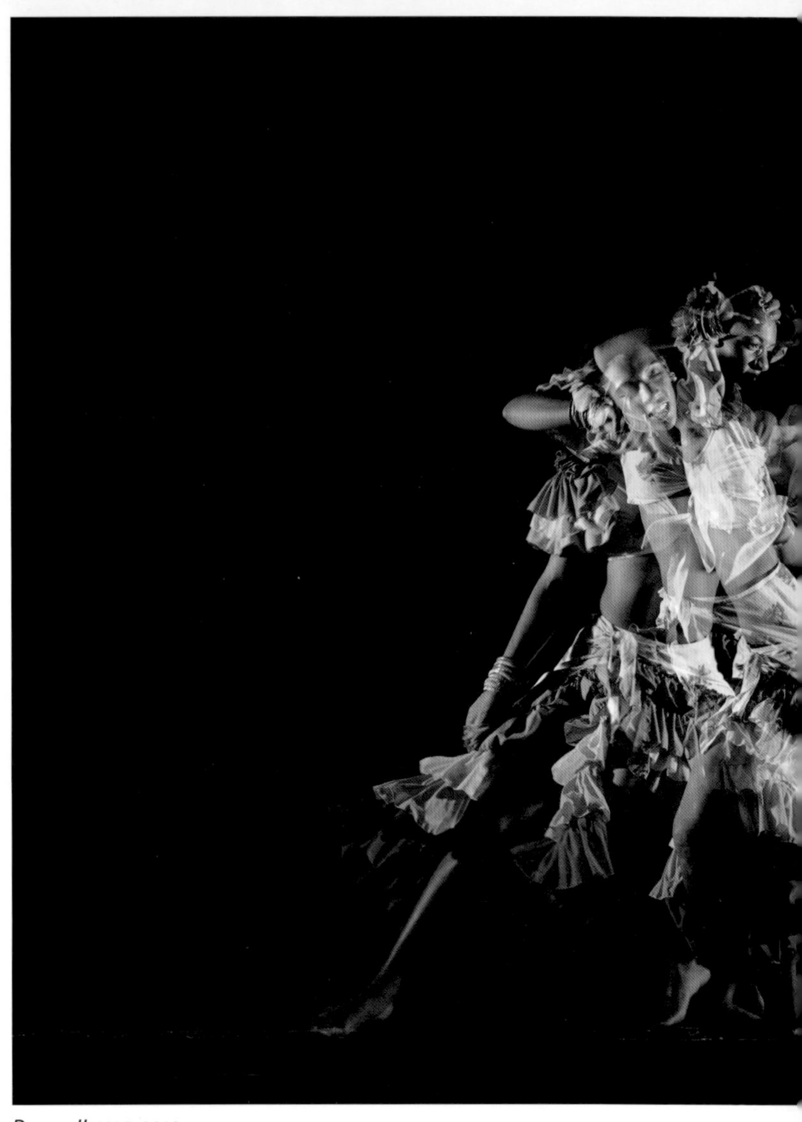

Dancer II, 1950, 2010

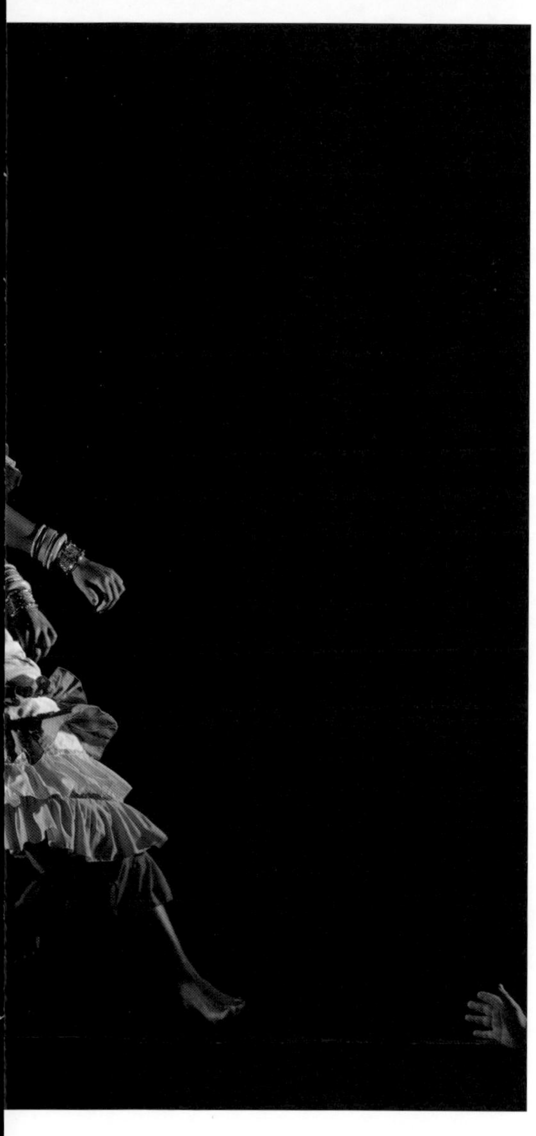

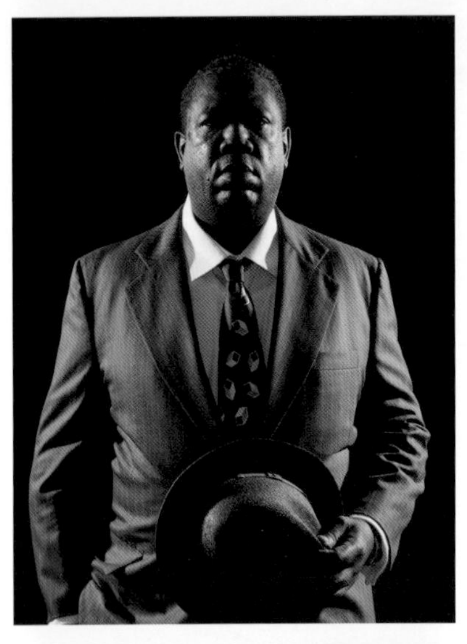

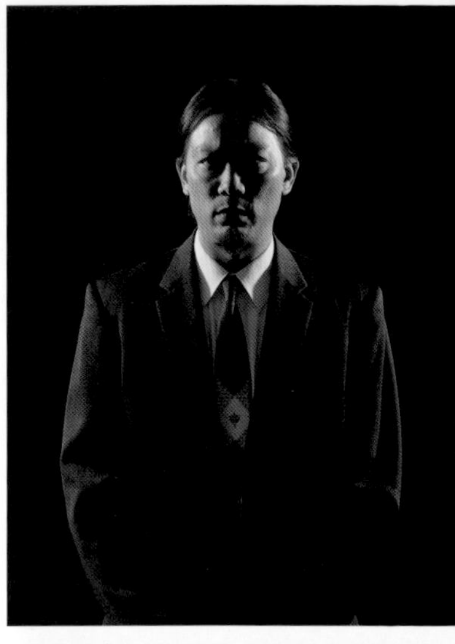

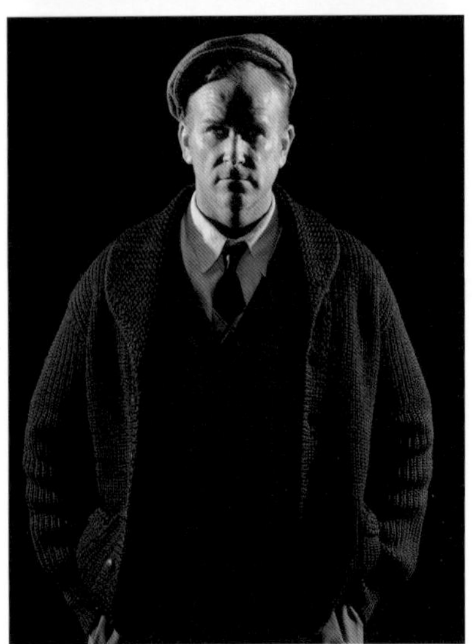

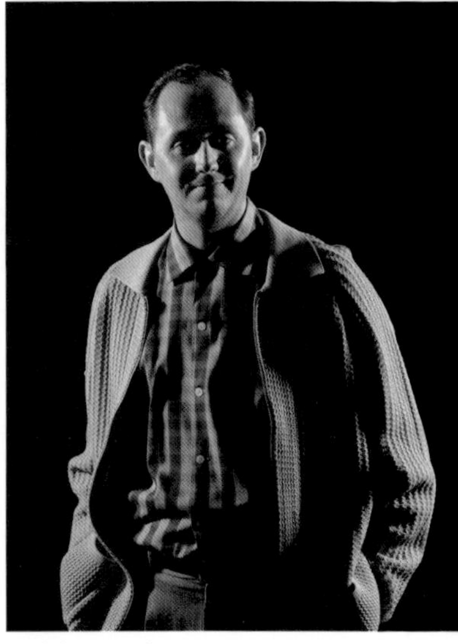

Malabar People: Bandleader, 1951, 2010

Malabar People: Cab Driver, 1951, 2010

Malabar People: Bouncer, 1951, 2010

Malabar People: Construction Worker, 1951, 2010

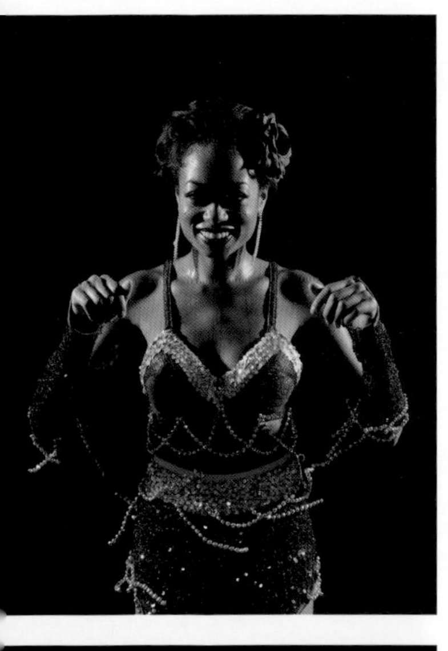

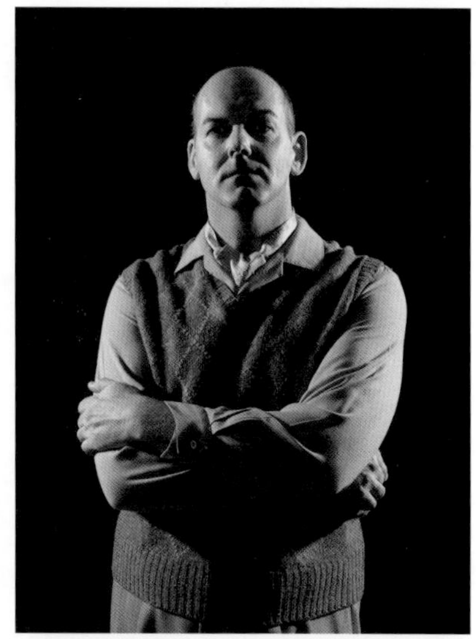

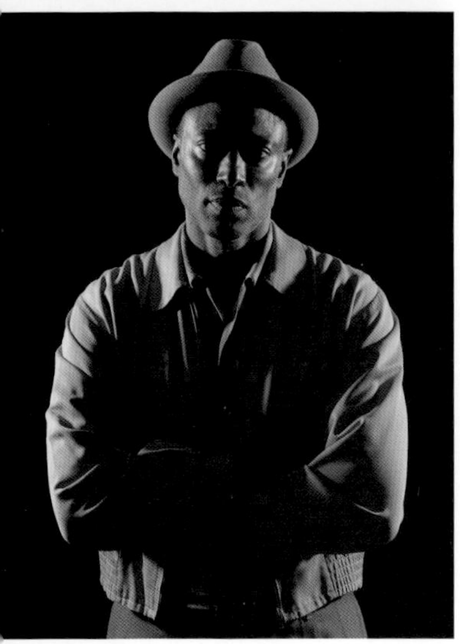

Malabar People:
Dancer*, *1951, 2010

Malabar People:
Logger*, *1951, 2010

Malabar People:
Female Impersonator*, *1951, 2010

Malabar People:
Longshoreman*, *1951, 2010

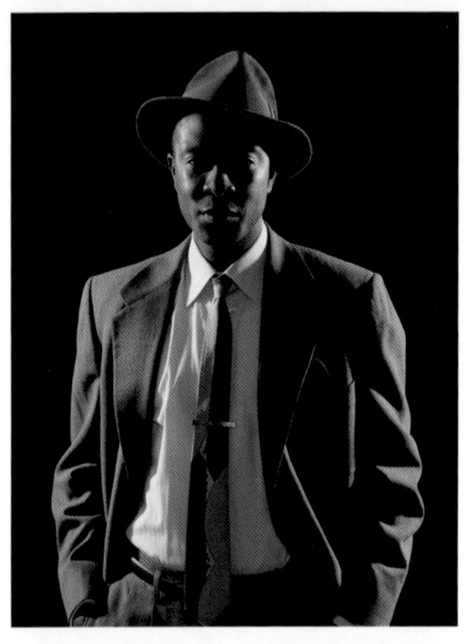

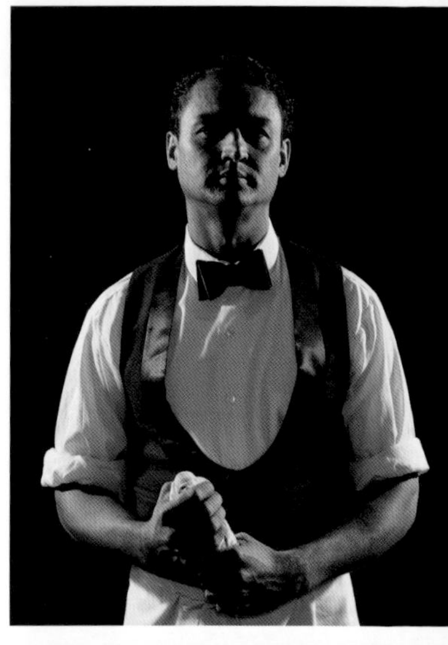

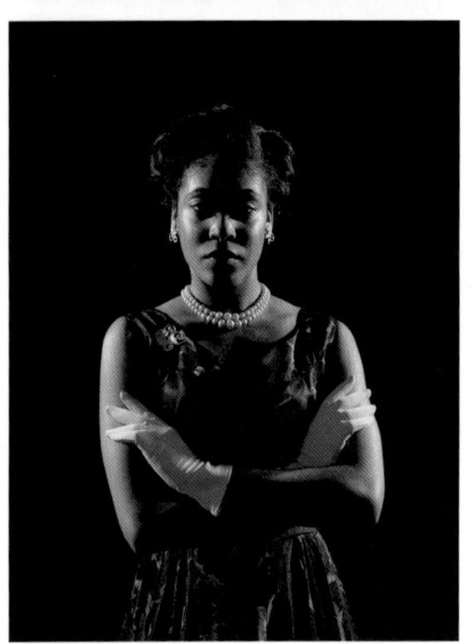

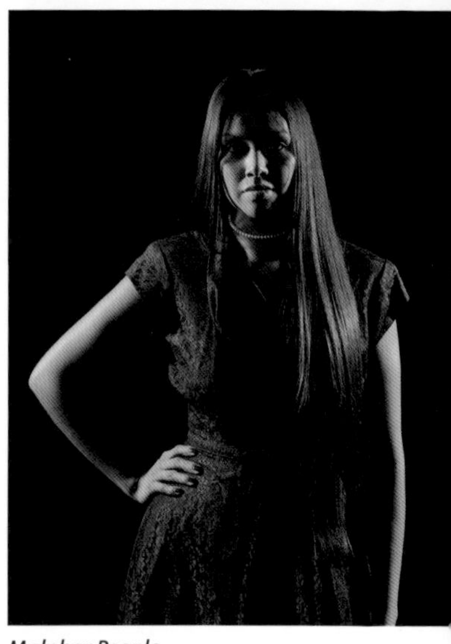

Malabar People:
Musician, 1951, 2010

Malabar People:
Owner/Bartender, 1951, 2010

Malabar People:
Single Woman I, 1951, 2010

Malabar People:
Single Woman II, 1951, 2010

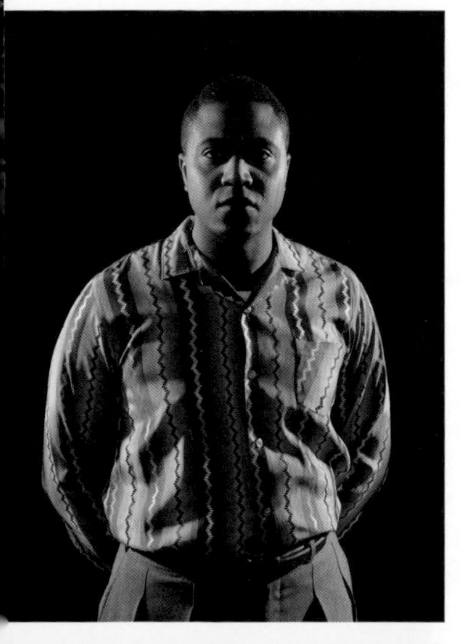

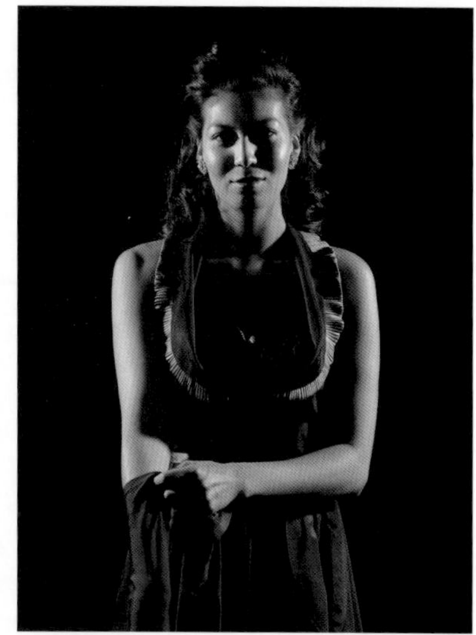

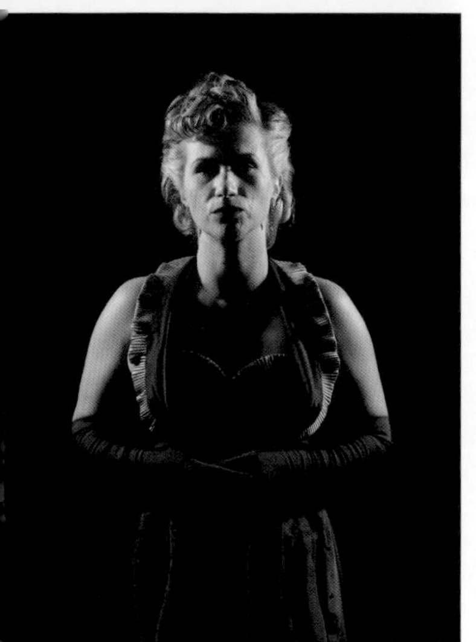

Malabar People: Student, 1951, 2010

Malabar People: Waitress I, 1951, 2010

Malabar People: Waitress II, 1951, 2010

Malabar People: West-Side Lady, 1951, 2010

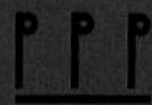

Introduction

A Backward Glance

Melanie O'Brian

WITH A BACKWARD GLANCE, Stan Douglas's entertainment chronicles approach complex realities in terms of history, the production of images and perception. The photographs in the exhibition *Entertainment: Selections from Midcentury Studio*[1] are an extension of the artist's practice of reexamining historic, site-specific layers, particularly the imaging of postwar North American[2] so-called *divertissements* from cabaret and carnival to sporting events. The work reveals the inherent theatricality in picture making and pulls the curtain back on sociopolitical contexts that not only coincide with a simultaneously specific and generalized post-war/post-recession optimism, but also conjure the darker ramifications entailed in looking back. This reader includes texts that offer insight into Douglas's exhibition. Considering the work in terms of remakes, nostalgia, objects of desire, magic, humour, and irony, the texts also approach the crucial relationship between the

[1] All works in *Midcentury Studio*, including *Malabar People*, are from 2010. The title of each work includes an indexical date, i.e. *Juggler, 1947*.

[2] Although the locations in *Entertainment* are not always revealed, the images were shot in Vancouver and belie a slippage between location and dislocation, specificity and generality. Douglas doesn't make location the subject, but instead applies aspects of Vancouver's history to a larger story of postwar optimism.

documentary and the fictional within debates around photography and contemporary art. They collectively position Douglas's work within a dialogue between photojournalistic objectivity and the fabrication of the image. This dialogue is one decisive point at issue in the work, while another crux is the subject of entertainment.

The title, *Entertainment*, suggests performance, hospitality and amusement, which, in a manner, Douglas delivers in his meticulous recreation (both in the studio and out) of midcentury scenes and social spaces as caught by the camera. In this project Douglas inhabits the character (or more specifically engages the photographic lens) of a fictional photographer who takes on various jobs — journalism to advertising — during the period from 1945 to 1951. In doing so he appears to perform the role of an earlier photographer, yet rather than undertaking theatre, he engages issues critical to contemporary art production and our current political and cultural climate. Achieving verisimilitude, Douglas reconstructed a studio using authentic period equipment as well as actors to produce staged photographs that emulate the period's obsession with *noir*-ish drama, trickery and magic, show business, sporting events, fashion, caught-in-the-moment scenes, and shifting technologies. A fetishization of technology could have been a pitfall here, but Douglas's digital large-scale prints avoid this. The sets are dramatic — strikingly lit in largely shadowy settings — the characters meticulously chosen, and the drama played out in the re-creation of the images. In *Entertainment*, the black-and-white images have a notable darkness to them, a closed off, even subterranean quality that conjures this drama, this cinematic view, but refers as well to the set-like space of the studio (even the outdoor scene of the *Cricket Pitch, 1951* is set against a dense, dark forest wall). The business of producing photographs differs vastly between this fictional midcentury picture taker and the picture maker Stan Douglas, giving rise to essential questions of the role of the image and the discursive spaces it occupies.

The connotation of entertainment within the critical spaces of art is largely derogatory; entertainment functions to distract or divert the viewer away from subjects of real significance. Douglas's work imbues the subject of entertainment with substance in its consideration of the gambits of performance for and with the camera, "entertaining" the idea of photography's place within entertainment's role in society. While performance and entertainment are not synonymous, both address audiences' wants and expectations. Douglas's images provide both the objects and spaces of entertainment and function as though re-performed from an archive. Physically enlarged — a scale consistent with contemporary art conventions — the reenacted scenes set up a slippage between the manipulated documentary moment and the studio. The referents and their translation belong to two separate cultural spheres of knowledge. One is under the auspices of journalism and "truth," and the other is under an intellectual questioning, within contemporary art, of that truth as it is found in the image. It is the performance of the documentary that leads the thinking on this work. This performance of the documentary occurs on two accounts — first in the original photographs that Douglas takes his cue from where we understand that the so-called objective representations of reality have been undermined by the subjective framing of the photographer; and second in Douglas's recreation of these images which operate on a set of principles found within a contemporary art discourse rather than in a journalistic or documentary one. In Douglas's work the means of representation are being measured and assessed, the production of images and narratives a performative layering of rhetoric, gesture, staging, and framing. The work in *Entertainment* reinvigorates the tension set up between the supposed autonomy of contemporary art and the lack of self-determination in the realms of journalism and mass media. While art appears to align itself with the discursive spaces of exhibitionality (the space of the exhibition), the documentary instead promotes exhibitionism.[3]

Social (and economic) systems of entertainment are revealed in the work. One understands the subcultures presented in Douglas's project to be part of these systems: the carnival, the cabaret, the hockey game, the cricket match, and the overall space of the nightclub. These are sites for diversion away from daily labour, the recent depression, and the more recent war, and they are sites that generate revenue, making up an entertainment economy that came into its own in the era pictured.[4] For example, *Entertainment* includes *Malabar People*,

[3] The notion of exhibitionality has been discussed by Okwui Enwezor in his contribution to the symposium *Berlin Documentary Forum 1*, 2010 and text "Documentary's Discursive Spaces," page 7 of the *Forum* guide. His thinking is indebted to Rosalind Krauss's essay "Photography's Discursive Spaces" in *The Originality of the Avant-Garde and Other Modernist Myths* (Cambridge: MIT Press, 1986).

[4] 1930-1948 is considered the Golden Age of Hollywood. Douglas conjures up the drama of Hollywood in *Midcentury Studio* (akin to Paramount, 20th Century Fox or Metro-Goldwyn-Mayer Studios). Today film and television — largely as entertainment in the diversion/propaganda sense — is as robust (or more so) as it was at a midcentury point.

portraits of the patrons and staff of a fictional early 1950s nightclub. The patrons range from upscale women to loggers, and the staff encompasses bartenders, waitresses and entertainers. Here the subjects, part of the nightclub subculture, reveal their collective potential for new orders or even resistance against societal norms. Douglas has made a diversity of ethnicity explicit in the nightclub images. This directorial casting encourages the viewer to take a closer look at the characters making up the cricket team or watching the hockey fight. Products of a distinctive politics of representation, these social spaces appear as shadowy frontiers of a sort and offer up possibilities of alternate systems.

Like Douglas's film work, which defies straightforward narrative expectation, the artist's photographs complicate linear reading yet remain, at their core, strong storytellers. The photographs in *Entertainment* collectively speak to notions of the reemployment of history and reproduction. Their indexicality is coded to the subcultures of entertainment and offer a partial portrait of a specific place and time as well as a sleight-of-hand around the articulation of the present. By looking back and re-engaging a postwar moment, Douglas's images speak to our current conditions. We might ask of this work, as Hal Foster does in *The Return of the Real*, "how does a *re*connection with a past practice support a *dis*connection from a present practice and/or a development of a new one?"[5]

---

[5] Hal Foster, *The Return of The Real* (Cambridge/London: MIT Press, 1999): x.

P P P

Midcentury Studio: Entertaining Stan Douglas's Photographic Remakes and Double Takes

Louis Kaplan

1. THINKING AROUND THE PREMISES.

In *Midcentury Studio*, Stan Douglas creates the fictional persona of a Vancouver photographer who is modeled in part on two larger-than-life predecessors both of whom made their mark during the golden age of tabloid photography and photojournalism. On the one hand, we have the legendary New Yorker, Weegee the Famous (Arthur Fellig), who transmuted crime and murder into a photographic art and a decent living, and who laced his images with a mordant sense of visual humour steeped in the tradition of Yiddish wit that laughs in the face of suffering, tragedy and death. On the other hand, there is the equally flamboyant Canadian aviator turned photojournalist Raymond Munro, who settled in Vancouver after the war where he teamed up with Art Jones to form the photo agency Artray Limited in 1948.[1] Interestingly enough, both of these midcentury characters wrote autobiographical narratives about their camera capers and other sensational exploits — *The Sky's No Limit* for the high-flying Munro and *Weegee by Weegee* for the self-aggrandizing Fellig.[2] Douglas's *Midcentury Studio* offers to the viewer a grand conceit in photographic simulation — mining and miming these and other news photographers by using period equipment and props as well as by capturing the look and style of the period in carefully staged black-and-white images. Each photo shoot in this series is likened to a theatrical production

---

[1] The Artray Limited Photographers Collection of about 11,000 photographs is held at the Vancouver Public Library. The collection is currently in the process of being digitized. For more information, see http://www.vpl.ca/artray/collection.html (7 October 2011).

[2] Raymond Z. Munro, *The Sky's No Limit* (Toronto: Key Porter Books, 1985); Arthur Fellig, *Weegee by Weegee: An Autobiography* (New York: Ziff-Davis Publishing, 1961).

enlisting the support of dozens of people. To achieve his goals, Douglas assembled a crew that included actors, dressers, camera assistants, set decorators, and makeup artists.

Douglas's imaginary photo reporter is cut from the same populist and versatile mould as these two real-life prototypes, and *Midcentury Studio* provides the viewer with a portfolio that includes a cross-section of the range of topical assignments that this photo hound might have covered in the period between 1945 and 1951. These human-interest stories range from crime scenes to novelty acts, from fashion and advertising shoots to sporting events. *Midcentury Studio*'s remakes even take up the multiple exposure strobe light effects that were pioneered by MIT scientist Harold Edgerton and his collaborator Gjon Mili. For example, *Dancer I, 1950* and *Dancer II, 1950* are in direct dialogue with Mili's stop motion portraits of the dancer Betty Bruce (1941). In Douglas's images, the viewer follows pivotal points in the flow of movement of an elaborately costumed black female dancer that enables a type of seeing where the camera surpasses the power of the naked eye. Structured like a pyramid in terms of its composition, *Dancer II, 1950* traces its twisting and gyrating choreography in the photographic tradition of a time-motion study.

Introducing the project, Douglas frames the life and times inhabited by his photographic alter ego in the following manner: "*Midcentury Studio* chronicles the career of a photographer who was introduced to his craft during the war and tried to make it into a business in the postwar period. It is also a fragmentary portrait of a North American city being normalized after a war."[3] The second sentence suggests to the reader that Douglas is also thinking about his own roots and how they are reflected in his project. His hometown of Vancouver plays a pivotal role in these images; this becomes most evident in the sixteen studio portraits known as *Malabar People, 1951*, to the extent that this series may function like a microcosm of the city and its diverse inhabitants.

2. AS TIME GOES BACK: REFLECTIONS ON NOSTALGIA.

Why this nostalgia for a midcentury photographic studio? Why the desire to fabricate Weegee's and Munro's worlds? Why the desire to transform the present into the seven years immediately following the end of World War II? There is little doubt that *Midcentury Studio* evokes nostalgia for a time when photojournalism and tabloid photography held a dominant position in the visual culture of Western societies. In taking up this fictitious photographic career, Douglas's retro remaking and remodeling project recalls that pinnacle moment when daily press photography ruled as the authoritative medium for the transmission of news, information and entertainment. Photographers such as Weegee or Munro were key players in the golden age of photojournalism and its mass dissemination of the photographic image. Nevertheless, the public's reliance on the picture press as mass visual medium would be supplanted by the

---

[3] Stan Douglas, "Midcentury Studio," in *Stan Douglas: Midcentury Studio*, ed. Tommy Simoens (Antwerp: Ludion, 2011), 7.

growth of television in the fifties. It can be said that we are even further removed from this photographic moment today given our digital visual culture and the convergence of media on the computer screen. In a similar manner, *Midcentury Studio* also expresses a longing for the analogical age of darkroom photography when society invested authority in the documentary image as the means by which to represent the truth of the world. As the condition of photography in the digital age has veered towards "photoshopping" and as the referent has become more subject to doubt in the questioning of its indexical validity, it is little wonder that there would be such a fascination with this earlier era for Douglas and other contemporary artists. However, the ironic twist of Douglas's belated gesture of retrofitting offers a paradoxical result in that it openly fabricates photographic fictions rather than reasserting documentary truths. In this highly staged manner, Douglas's nostalgic images return to the past in order to further entertain the distance and disjunction between then and now.

Douglas's conscious restaging of scenes from the 1940s and early 1950s is not an isolated exercise and one can find other contemporary photographic projects in the same nostalgic vein over the past decade including a few that return to Weegee's world in particular. One thinks of the recent exhibition of David McDermott and Peter McGough and their restaging of classic photographs from Man Ray, Paul Outerbridge, Irving Penn, and others in order to simulate the photographic world of glossy magazines circa 1955. In *Of Beauty and Being* (2010), the two artists deploy the obsolete technology of tricolour carbon printing to stage nineteen works that mime the look of that period.[4] Meanwhile, Barbara Hammer's *History Lessons* (2001) restages Weegee's crime scene photographs of the 1940s using contemporary female performers in an effort to question the gender hierarchies that are inherent to such images.[5] Finally, Melanie Pullen's *High Fashion Crime Scenes* (2005) takes its inspiration from Luc Sante's book *Evidence*[6] and from vintage crime scene photographs found in the archives of Los Angeles Police Department. Similar to Douglas, her elaborate fabrications employ up to sixty persons for any given shoot. However, most of Pullen's images are shot in colour with their female models dressed in the stylish fashions of today. Pullen states her objectives as follows: "I took this horrific subject and turned it into something aesthetic."[7] The aestheticizing tendency that binds together these projects reflects upon our contemporary moment, which seeks not just to pay homage and/or parody the past, but also to fetishize and reframe it as an art object. In this way, the various works in *Midcentury Studio* are to be understood as objects of desire and as artful commodities to which a nostalgic noir lustre have

---

[4] The exhibition took place at Cheim & Read Gallery in New York from 7 January to 12 February 2011. For a complete set of images, please visit the artists' website: www.mcdermottandmcgough.com/photography/ofbeautyandbeing/index.php (7 October 2011).

[5] Hammer confides that she "wanted to use Weegee's photographs but...didn't have a copyright for them." See her interview with Michelle Handelman in *indieWIRE* from 25 October 2001. http://www.indiewire.com/article/interview_barbara_hammer_teaches_and_titillates_with_history_lessons/ (7 October 2011).

[6] Luc Sante, *Evidence* (New York: Farrar Straus and Giroux, 1992). The project looks at fifty-five crime scene photographs shot during the years 1914 and 1918.

[7] Melanie Pullen is quoted from an interview with Jessica Hundley, "Fashion Victims," *Los Angeles Times* (Calendar), 7 June 2004. For the complete set of crime scene images, visit her website: http://www.melaniepullen.com/ (7 October 2011).

accrued. Given Douglas's double takes, press images now return as art photographs.[8]

3. HUMOUR AND IRONY.

Midcentury Studio follows on the heels of an earlier video and photography project by Douglas in 2008 entitled *Crowds and Riots*. Included in the exhibition "Humor, Irony and the Law,"[9] his project includes four large-scale photographs of places associated with historical events in Vancouver involving civic unrest. Moving across four critical episodes (dated 1912, 1935, 1955, and 1971) Douglas's reenactments are, in certain respects, direct predecessors of his current body of remakes. It is possible to argue that any type of photographic restaging or doubling engages in humor and irony to some extent because of a need to parody the original. In the case of *Midcentury Studio*, this is certainly the case in those evocative works that directly quote from the great Weegee's ghost.[10] It is as if Douglas has superimposed a

[8] The return of press photographs as art commodities has angered one devoted Weegee blogger, who complained that "in his entire life Weegee probably never made what it costs to be a single Weegee influenced, staged photograph." This post was written in direct response to the exhibition of Douglas's images at the David Zwirner Gallery in March 2011. See: http://weegeeweegeeweegee.blogspot.com/2011/03/father-was-waiting-to-meet-us.html (7 October 2011). While it may be a natural impulse to criticize Douglas's stylized project for aestheticizing the subjects of everyday news photography, things are more complicated when we remember that Weegee thought of himself first and foremost as an artist and that one of his proudest achievements was the exhibition of his images at the Museum of Modern Art.

[9] The exhibition takes its title from a 1967 essay by Gilles Deleuze as part of his work on the question of masochism. The exhibition took place at David Zwirner, New York from 30 October to 23 December 2008.

[10] There is another layer of irony in the fact that the press release for the artist's exhibition pointed to the relationship between Douglas and Weegee in a most peculiar way adding the letter "r" and thereby changing the meaning drastically with this slip of the pen. The text reads: "Douglas's midcentury alter-ego revokes the career of the legendary photographer Arthur Fellig, also known as Weegee (1899-1968)." http://www.davidzwirner.com/resources/67435/2011%20SD%20Press%20Release%20FINAL.pdf (7 October 2011).

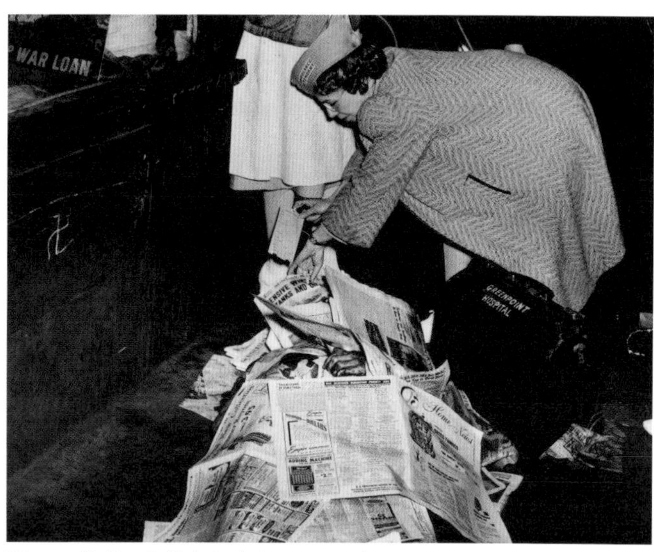

Weegee (Arthur Fellig), ***Ambulance Attendant Tagging Corpse***, 1943
Collection of the International Center of Photography/Getty Images

deadpan layer of Conceptual comedy and black humour over Weegee's own inimical style in images that fake or parody death such as *Burlap, 1948* or *Incident, 1949*. These image simulations offer macabre looks at murder victims whose bodies have been covered in burlap or newspaper. The first image gives the nod to Weegee's *Body under a Blanket* (1942), while the second image directly quotes from two of Weegee's classic crime scenes — *Joy of Living* (1945) and *Ambulance Tagging a Corpse* (1943). In the former image, the unconscious automatism of Weegee's camera catches the movie marquee announcement of the film, *Joy of Living*, in front of the corpse, illustrating his mordant wit via this word and image interplay. There is further humour in the fact that these victims are wrapped up in the very medium that serves to disseminate their sensational stories and their gruesome demise. While feigning death, Douglas's version cannot resist repeating this gesture as well as adding another ironic touch to the scene in that the police investigator appears to be reading the newspaper while on the job.

Another cluster of playful and humorous images illustrates scenes from the fictional photographer's visit to a carnival in 1946. The artist's series of popular entertainments includes *Passe-tête, 1946*; *Juggler, 1946*; and *Clown, 1946*. There is levity in *Passe-tête, 1946* as it offers a self-reflexive statement on photographic fabrication and simulation itself. By slipping his head into the scene of the action, the carnival-goer takes up the subject position of the Wild West sheriff who shoots down the bad guy in front of the cardboard saloon. Here, the non-Anglo ethnicity of the man in sheriff's clothing offers a playful subversion of conventional racial stereotypes. Two of these images portray juggling as a visual entertainment. In *Clown, 1946* a bug-eyed circus performer has been caught in the act of juggling three oranges. Finally, one witnesses the black humor of the one-legged female juggler of knives in an image that helps to recall the intimate relationship between carnival and the vulnerability of the flesh.

There is an interesting tension in Douglas's project between the unrehearsed quality of the original spot newspaper photographs and their restaging as highly theatrical images that tend, in many cases, to repress photography's automatism in their nuanced choreography. Yet, this type of tension is exactly what generates the overarching humour and irony of *Midcentury Studio*.

Another way to put this point would be to say that there is laughter in the gap between contingency and contrivance. This points to how Douglas's fabricated and belated images can never qualify as documentary photographs.[11]

In sharp contrast to the rhetoric of the "decisive moment" that guided the photojournalism of this period, Douglas's remakes make their mark as art and artifice. *Midcentury Studio* also answers the concerns about photographic automatism that in the 1940s and 1950s was "one of the primary arguments against photography being regarded as legitimate art form."[12] The artist does this by staging an elaborate series of photographic fictions that are willing to entertain a degree of both humor and irony.

4. MALABAR PEOPLE.

Douglas's *Malabar People* series offers an interesting case study in aesthetic sociology. The primary source and inspiration for these sixteen artistic portraits lies in an actual piece of sociological research, "The Social System of a Vancouver Nightclub" written by the artist's uncle, Laurence F. Douglas. This organizational analysis reviews the social relations and "the patterns of interaction prevalent in a Vancouver nightclub."[13] Laurence Douglas's code name for this nightclub in the thesis is the Malabar and the author proceeds to offer

---

[11] This does not rule out the possibility that the documentary source images might also be subject to certain aspects of stagecraft.

[12] Douglas, "Midcentury Studio," 6.

[13] Laurence Douglas, "The Social System of a Vancouver Nightclub: An Illustration of a Method of Analysis of an Organisation – A Preliminary Study of the Patterns of Interaction Prevalent in a Vancouver Nightclub" (B.A. Thesis, University of British Columbia, 1960).

a thoroughgoing investigation and systematic analysis of this local establishment and how it functions as an entertainment provider. The essay offers a variety of insights on such topics as social organization, deviant behavior and race and ethnic relations. In transforming this sociological treatise into artistic practice, Douglas imagines what would have happened if his midcentury photographer had visited the Malabar in 1951 and had taken studio portraits of some of the key members inhabiting this subculture. One can think of these portraits as constituting an ideal typology, with one-half of them devoted to the patrons frequenting this establishment and the other half devoted to those working at the nightclub. Laurence Douglas refers to the entertainers of the Malabar as "singers, comedians, female impersonators, dancers and drummers."[14] Meanwhile, Stan Douglas focuses on four of them in his portrait series — a bandleader, a musician, a female impersonator, and a dancer.

One of the most striking things about *Malabar People* is the ethnic and racial diversity of its subjects. The nightclub as a source of entertainment functions as a social magnet, attracting people from many walks of life as well as from diverse backgrounds. The leisure activities of music and dance forge a loose community of various social and ethnic types who normally would not meet anywhere else. Both the clientele and the employees are not at all reflective of the dominant model of Anglo-Canadian identity constituted by white English-speaking

[14] Ibid., 13.

Protestants of that era. In a sense, this heterogeneous group of people anticipates the contemporary multicultural model of Canadian identity. As Laurence Douglas specifies, "The social system of the Malabar is comprised of persons who are members of several ethnic groups. Thus the owner-manager is an East Indian, his wife is White, his employees are native Indians, Whites, Negroes and East Indians, and his customers present this same picture of ethnic differentiation."[15] Douglas's photographs have translated this "picture of ethnic differentiation" from sociological study to portrait studio and added a few more ethnically diverse representatives along the way. For instance, while the thesis does not mention any Chinese employees at the Malabar, Douglas portrays the *Bouncer, 1951*, as a Chinese-Canadian male in his thirties. Given the fact that the Malabar was "located in the East End of Vancouver on the fringe of the area popularly known as Chinatown,"[16] this casting choice does not seem fanciful at all.

The standard format of the composition of these photographs also creates an equalizing tendency for the people who have the Malabar in common. It does not matter whether we are looking at *Waitress I, 1951* or *West-Side Lady, 1951*. In either case, the female subject stands and directly faces the camera lit by two spotlights, against a black backdrop. There is a noirish atmosphere to this series that bathes these figures in deep shadows except for a few highlights that bring out the foreheads

---

[15] Ibid., 116.

[16] Ibid., 12. According to Stan Douglas, "Malabar is a pseudonym, probably for the New Delhi Café." Stan Douglas to Melanie O'Brian, e-mail, 26 August 2011.

and cheekbones of the *Malabar People*. These nocturnal portraits typically leave the eyes in mystery. Such subdued lighting verging on darkness alludes to the fact that these portraits are of people who are associated with a nightclub, and a "specialized deviant sub-culture"[17] engaged in a number of activities (e.g., bootlegging, drugs, prostitution) that do not care to see the light of day. As Laurence Douglas writes: "In treating deviant behavior, the Malabar is regarded as a delinquent social system, a 'protest organization' in which the management has instituted some illegitimate practices in order to maintain the establishment as an ongoing system and has given tacit approval of some others."[18] In contrast to this description, as idealizing remakes and double takes the stylized portraits stress dignity over delinquency.

5. MAGIC PHOTOS.

Three images in the *Midcentury Studio* series involve magic tricks. In this imaginary photographic oeuvre, *Smoke, 1947*; *Rings, 1947*; and *Flame, 1947* are presented to the viewer as a series derived from 1947. Featuring the tricks of the magician's trade, these images ask the viewer a pointed question: Do you believe in magic? *Smoke, 1947* is an odd and ironic image that features an indexical finger pointing at a disappearing act, something that appears to have gone up in smoke already. It is again not a case of a Magnum decisive moment. As Douglas comments, it is more about "getting the wrong moment" and of "giving an image of having just missed

[17] Ibid., 125.

[18] Ibid., 13.

whatever was in the smoke's place."[19] Not unlike the photograph, the smoke functions here as the physical trace of a vanished referent. In any event, the pointing finger registers photography's indexical status as it frames "whatever" and as it captures the image, whether right or wrong. *Rings, 1947* provides more sleights of hand as the magician is photographed going through the motions of an "impossible-looking combination of rings."[20] Finally, *Flame, 1947* offers what appears to be an incidence of spontaneous combustion in the process of bursting forth from the magician's hand. All three images bring to the forefront the question of whether seeing is believing. This is a question shared by both the photographer's and the magician's art. On the one hand, the skeptic refuses to believe, whether dealing with the sleight of a photographic or a magical hand. This is especially the case in our era marked as it is by digital photography and Photoshop manipulations. On the other hand, these seductive images, with their veneer of a documentary record, encourage one to believe in the truth of what has been recorded before the lens. In other words, one is tempted to believe in magic and in the magic of photography.

From an even broader perspective, Douglas's attraction to magic in these finely crafted and crafty images can be viewed as emblematic of the nature of photography itself. One recalls in this context William Henry Fox Talbot's reflections on the photographic

---

[19] See the transcript of the interview with David Balzer conducted on 11 April 2011. It is entitled "Q. and A.: Stan Douglas on *Midcentury Studio*." http://davidkbalzer.com/criticism-journalism/stan-douglas-on-midcentury-studio/ (7 October 2011).

[20] "Q. and A.: Stan Douglas on *Midcentury Studio*," (7 October 2011).

process and its evocation of a new type of magic. As the British inventor wrote at the advent of photography in 1839: "A person unacquainted with the process, if told that nothing of all this was executed by the hand, must imagine that one has at one's call the genius of Aladdin's lamp. And, indeed, it may almost be said that this is something of the same kind. It is a little bit of magic realized, of natural magic."[21] Weegee echoes Talbot's thoughts, though in a less refined manner, when he makes an analogy between his beloved Speed Graphic camera and the magic lantern of Aladdin. "It's like a modern Aladdin's lamp. You rub it — in this case, the camera — you push the button and it gives you the things you want."[22] In this light, Stan Douglas's *Smoke, 1947* might be the direct result of letting the genie out of the camera lamp.

6. SPORTS ENTERTAINMENTS.

Midcentury Studio also takes up two other popular entertainments through large-format images that are made at the end of our photographer's career — *Hockey Fight, 1951* and *Cricket Pitch, 1951*. In turning to hockey and cricket as his photographic subject matter, Douglas stages postwar scenes related to two of Canada's most important pastimes. In the first image, we bear witness to the violent passions unleashed by the hockey game. It goes without saying that hockey serves as a crucial

[21] William Henry Fox Talbot, "Letter of 30 January 1839," in *Literary Gazette*, 2 February 1839.

[22] This quotation is taken from Weegee's audio interview for the LP "Famous Photographers Tell How" that was released in 1958. It is also interesting to point out that Weegee dedicates his autobiography to his camera invoking the same metaphor of the Aladdin's lamp.

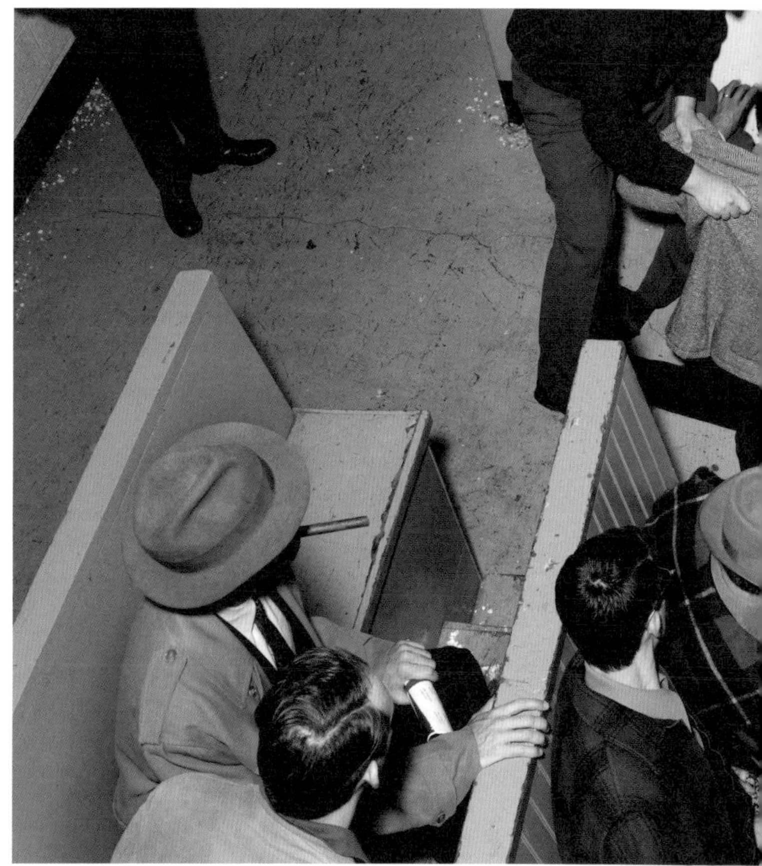

Stan Douglas, *Hockey Fight, 1951*, 2010

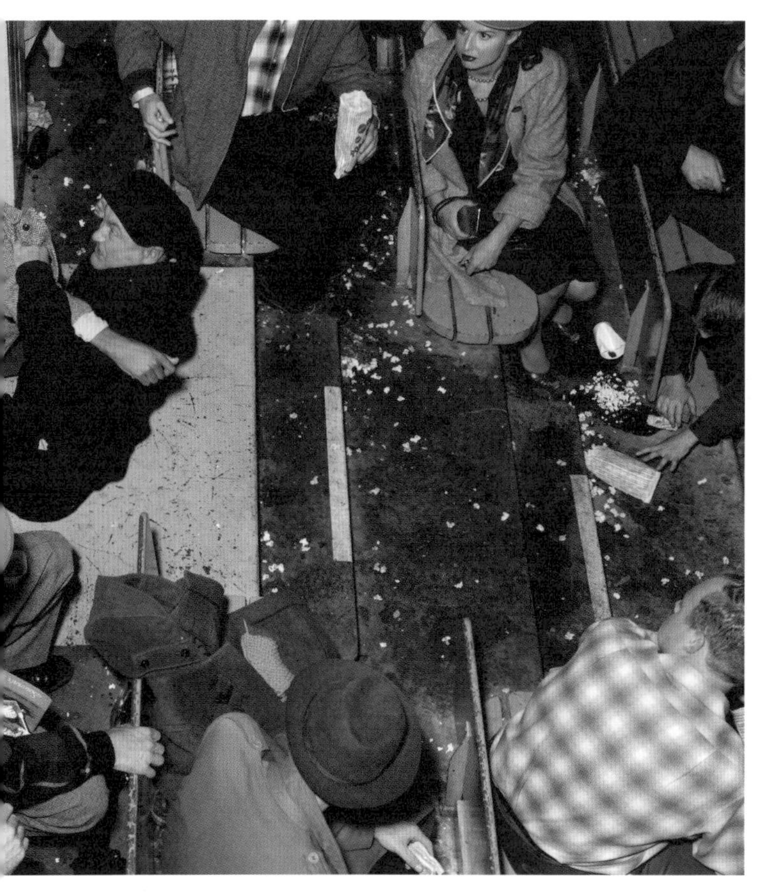

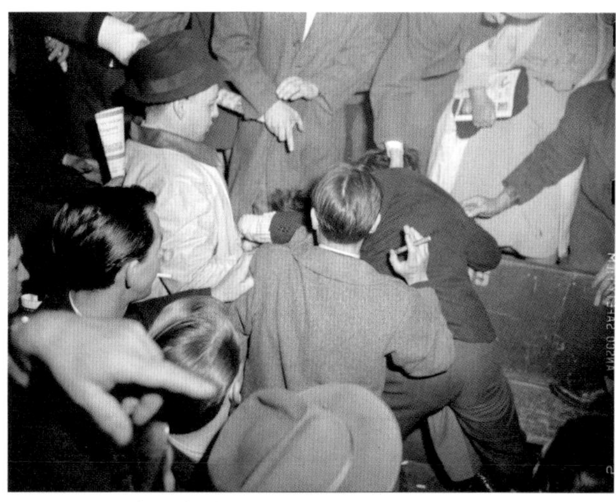

Ray Munro, *Fight at hockey game at Forum, Canucks vs Skyhawks*, 1948
Collection of the Vancouver Public Library, VPL 84088D

point of reference for national pride and that it provides a bond for Canadian being-in-common. But this image illustrates how things can get out of hand among the home and native audience. *Hockey Fight* wears its humour on its jersey sleeve in that it focuses the viewer's attention away from the ice where one would normally expect to be entertained by fisticuffs among the players. Instead, we are transported to the grandstands via a bird's-eye view where a fight has broken out between two spectators. It so happens that there is a direct and hometown newspaper source for Douglas's *Hockey Fight, 1951*. It is a photograph snapped by Munro entitled *Fight at hockey game at Forum, Canucks vs.* [San Diego] *Skyhawks* from 16 April 1948. Munro took his photograph during the inaugural year of this indoor arena built to house the Vancouver Canucks, who were at that time playing in the now defunct Pacific Coast Hockey League. In staging this photographic remake at the Kerrisdale Arena (another old hockey rink still in use), Douglas's image hearkens back to a bygone era. Situated in the press booth, the overhead vantage point and wider shot allow for a more direct look at the fight in progress in comparison with Munro's photograph. Another lovely period touch in Douglas's nostalgic staging is the use of fedora hats, one of which is tipped at the almost exact angle as the one in the lower portion of the Munro.

While one thinks of hockey as *the* national sport of Canada today, it should be recalled that the first Prime Minister of Canada declared otherwise. Sir John A. MacDonald and his cabinet bestowed that honour and distinction upon cricket in the very year of Confederation in 1867. The game has been particularly active in British Columbia from the mid-nineteenth century. The Afro-Canadian Douglas comments on this multicultural game from a post-colonialist perspective in noting that the players are "descendent of all regions of the British empire."[23] In contrast to the interior view of *Hockey Fight, 1951* with its focus on the two rowdy spectators, *Cricket Pitch, 1951* takes the viewer to the great outdoors, right onto the field focusing on the players with the photographer immersed in the action. From the field-level vantage point of the cricket pitch, it is possible to observe the two batsmen on offense as well as most of the fielding team wearing their white period uniforms. With the cricket field set in a park surrounded by statuesque

[23] Douglas is quoted here in Christopher Phillips, "The Adventure of a Photographer," in *Stan Douglas: Midcentury Studio*, ed. Tommy Simoens (Antwerp: Ludion, 2011), 15.

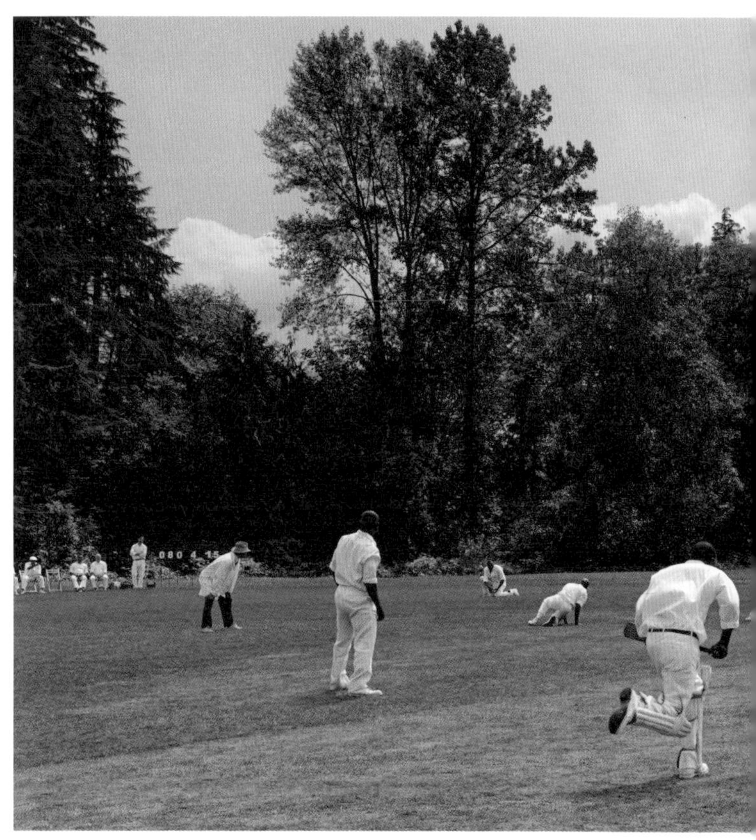

Stan Douglas, *Cricket Pitch, 1951*, 2010

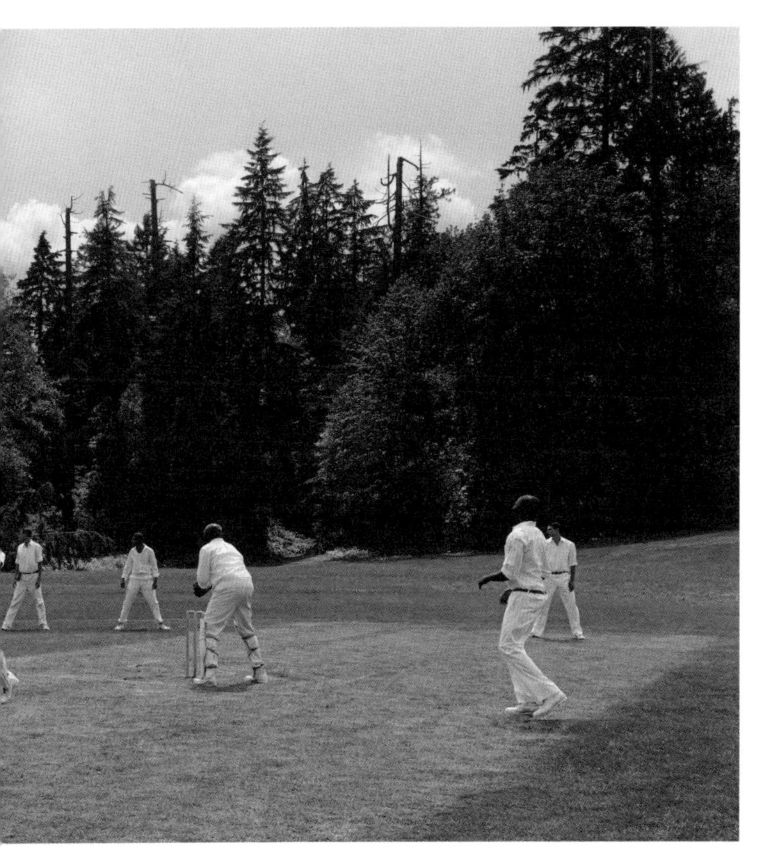

trees and with its wide horizontal expanse, this panoramic image also alludes to the genre of landscape photography. *Cricket Pitch* creates an interesting tension between nature and culture as this team sport rooted in the British Empire is played against the natural backdrop of receding Canadian woods.[24]

7. TIME OUT.

In 1950, Douglas's imaginary photographer shot a diptych entitled *Watch, 1950*. It is a "before" and "after" image used as an illustration for a story on how to steal a watch — how a thief can separate an unsuspecting victim from his timepiece. What looks like a friendly handshake turns out to be a hostile action against the dupe's wristwatch. Douglas remarks that such a sequence would serve as an illustration to an article "warning you about shaking hands with the wrong person."[25] In terms of the overarching strategies of the *Midcentury Studio* project, *Watch, 1950* offers an apt symbol for Douglas's photographic remakes and double takes that seek to turn back the hands of time. These entertaining images take us out of the present and transport us back to another time. Douglas's is a nostalgic gesture cast out against a contemporary moment measured in digital time, and one that seeks a return to the camera as an analogue clock

---

[24] There is a photograph by Art Jones of a *Cricket Match at Brockton Oval* between Ontario and British Columbia dated 4 August 1948 that appears to be one of the sources for this image (VPL Accession Number 84179).

[25] "Q. and A.: Stan Douglas on *Midcentury Studio*" (7 October 2011).

for seeing.[26] Our watches have been stolen away by a photographer who may be likened to a thief of time. But unlike the case of the midcentury watch thief, we welcome being caught in this act.

[26] Here I allude to Barthes's metaphorical phrasing that "cameras, in short, were clocks for seeing." See Roland Barthes, *Camera Lucida: Reflections on Photography*, trans. Richard Howard (New York: Hill and Wang, 1981), 15.

The Magical Realism of Postwar America:

On Entertainment: Selections from Midcentury Studio

Maria Muhle

"'Photography-as-art,' says Sascha Stone, 'is a very dangerous field.'"[1]

| Walter Benjamin

STAN DOUGLAS'S BLACK-AND-WHITE IMAGES from *Midcentury Studio* enact the foundational myth of photography: automatism (i.e. its technical capacity to automatically and therefore neutrally and objectively register reality through the camera). The project, which includes the portrait series *Malabar People*, addresses two main oppositions that unfold out of the technical character of photography and inhabit it from its beginnings. First, the struggle between photography and painting, and the discussion of "photography-as-art;" second, the more contemporary reformulation of this discussion in the opposition between documentary and fictional images, and the dissolution of this opposition in the recent strategies of fictionalization or the staging of alleged "documents" (from the photojournalist perspective) or "snapshots" (from the artistic) — a dissolution that points at the always problematic status of the notions of objectivity and authenticity in relation to the photographic image.

[1] Quoted in Walter Benjamin, "Little History of Photography," in *Selected Writings, 1931-1934*, vol. II.2, (Boston: Harvard University Press, 2005), 526.

Midcentury Studio develops against the backdrop of the narrative of a fictitious photographer who gets involved with photography more or less by accident and without any prior familiarity with artistic photography or any other kind of visual art.[1] This is the premise from which *Midcentury Studio* operates, as the photojournalist works on news images, takes pictures of everyday events for the press, and undertakes jobs in advertising photography. The *Midcentury Studio* images are thus historical re-creations of a specific postwar moment and its atmosphere.

The images in *Entertainment: Selections from Midcentury Studio* are mostly portraits — a female juggler, a clown, a young man behind a *passe-tête* picturing a cowboy, a dancer in motion — but the exhibition also includes two North American "genre scenes" — a scene from a cricket pitch and a fight in the stands during a hockey game — as well as the representation of magic tricks. In *Malabar People*, following Douglas's story, he portrays, against a black backdrop that can be read as a reference to Weegee's nocturnal images, workers and patrons of the fictional postwar Malabar nightclub in Vancouver. He assembles a tentative archive of the different characters frequenting the club, from the West-Side Lady, the Student or the Longshoreman to the Cab Driver, the Logger, the Bouncer or the Musician, the Waitress and the Dancer. While the images of the first series focus more specifically on singular aspects of

[1] "*Midcentury Studio* chronicles the career of a photographer who was introduced to his craft during the war and tried to make it into a business in the postwar period. It is also a fragmentary portrait of a North American city being normalized after a war." Stan Douglas, "Midcentury Studio," in *Stan Douglas: Midcentury Studio*, ed. Tommy Simoens (Antwerp: Ludion, 2011), 7.

entertainment — magic tricks, circus acts or sport events — the images of the latter present the archive of the shady world of the nightclub and function as an allegory, or "fragmentary portrait," of the postwar struggle of any North American city on its way back to "normality."[2]

AUTOMATIC ACCIDENTS

Douglas explores the automatism of these photographic images in two directions that at first seem contradictory. On the one hand, they manage to enact the essential skill of photography inasmuch as they suspend time; they capture reality by freezing a specific moment. This becomes apparent on a formal level through the use of lighting that accentuates the instantaneous character of each image, and on the level of content through the use of suspended flying objects — a knife and an orange in the juggling images — and through the suspension of time in the magic trick, fight and cricket game images.[3]

This immediacy is the hypothesis of the photographic genre recreated by Douglas: the Weegee-style, 1950s, crime reporter documentary photograph, with an aspiration to be objective, neutral and true, and a reliance on the assumption that your camera (i.e. its automatism) does the work. In Weegee's practice *in the field*, in mid-century North American reality, this translates into "his preternatural ability to arrive at the scene of crime moments after its commission,"[4] — the immediacy

[2] Ibid.

[3] What also becomes apparent is the classical opposition between cinema as the technique of setting images in motion ("living" images) and photography as the suspension of time and its internal relation to death (as Roland Barthes theorizes).

[4] Douglas, "Midcentury Studio," 6.

of the images reinforcing their relation to reality, their "truthfulness."

But the automatism of the camera does something other than produce a regulated relation between reality and its image through the recording process. The suppression of the photographer-as-author through the mechanical device produces a paradoxical result as there is always something out of control, unintentional, accidental, or as Douglas puts it in his description of Weegee's photographic style: there are always "uncanny events at the periphery of the images that were beyond his [Weegee's] control and automatically recorded by the apparatus."[5]

What Douglas suggests, and what his images explore, is that these two qualities — the immediacy of the image and its uncontrolled elements — are fundamentally linked within photography. Or, put differently, the loss of control is not contingent (and so needs to be brought under control), but is necessarily inscribed within the technique of photography, within its automatism. Therefore photography does not provide an especially *realistic* image of the world, but rather an especially *aleatory* one — an image that is the result of technical skills that deploy an aesthetic potential, not by obeying an intentional principle but by allowing for the unforeseeable, the uncontrolled, for a specific form of aesthetic freedom of changes and processes that do not obey a teleological order.

---

[5] Ibid.

This growing doubt about the naturalistic capacities of photography is thereby "the idiom" of the images of *Midcentury Studio*. The "automatism" of the camera, Douglas claims, cannot be understood beyond its "inherent Surrealism" — or beyond Henri Cartier-Bresson's affirmation of "artistic agency based on the quasi-mystical notion of a 'decisive moment.'"[6] The discussion about photography-as-art is internally rearticulated through this opposition between a pure automatism, as the (impossible) *desideratum* of the "realist" interpretation of photography, and another form of automatism in which the creative momentum (a momentum of loss of control, of surrealism, a surplus of reality within the image, the properly aesthetic momentum) is always already inscribed and that is — on the content level — paradigmatically addressed through the "playful" dimension in the selected images. The notion of "entertainment" featured in the title of the exhibition assumes in this context a closeness to the aesthetic logic of the "free play" by insisting on the dimension of the "accidental," the "unforeseeable," the "contingent."

PHOTOGRAPHY-AS-MAGIC

The photographic automatism is hence presented as "adulterated," it is not sheer mechanical representation of reality (an accurate reflection of nature), but always

[6] The artist attributes this assumption of a pure automatism of photography to the photoconceptualism of the 1970s as well as to recent varieties of neo-pictorialism. See Douglas, "Midcentury Studio," 6.

comprises a Surrealist element, something beyond control, something that is not completely absorbed into the realistic equation: an excess of reality within the representation. And this excessive or aleatory character of photography is not the subjective — or creative — intervention of the author in the process of photography; it actually *derives* from its automatism. Already André Bazin, in his seminal analysis "The Ontology of the Photographic Image" (1945), articulates the opposition between painting and photography through the automatism of the latter, which he traces back to Alberti and the discovery of central-perspective (Bazin calls this "the original sin of Western painting"[7]). There he defines automatism in a very specific — aesthetic — way. The difference between painting and photography is *not* the degree of realistic representation (he admits that a drawing can give far more information than a photograph), but its *automaticity*, as "for the first time, between the originating object and its reproduction there intervenes only the instrumentality of a nonliving agent. For the first time an image of the world is formed automatically, without the creative intervention of man."[8] The blank space, left vacant by the author — the creative intervention of man — is now occupied by the magic or irrational factions of the photographic apparatus:

[7] André Bazin, "The Ontology of the Photographic Image," in *Film Quarterly*, Vol. 13, No. 4. (Summer, 1960): 4-9; on p. 7 Bazin explains how Alberti and the discovery of central-perspective allows for an objective reproduction of the real world and its transposition onto the canvas through geometric calculations. It is thus an automatism *avant la lettre* and therefore opposed to traditional painting that depends on the perception of the painter. It is therefore doomed to subjectivism and relativism, only the automatic registration and reproduction guarantees an objective, unadulterated image of reality "as it is."

[8] Ibid.

"Photography enjoys a certain advantage in virtue of this transference of reality from the thing to its reproduction." This advantage is the "irrational power of the photograph to bear away our faith."[9]

The discussion about realism that seems to dominate the discussion about "photography-as-art" is thus replaced by this "transference of reality" that no longer addresses the resemblance between images and reality, but rather their technical genealogy: the fact that they were *not* made by man — they are "traces," as Georges Didi-Huberman points out.[10] Along similar lines, Roland Barthes claims that "the realists do not take the photograph for a 'copy' of reality, but for an emanation of *past reality*: a magic, not an art,"[11] and refers to the same tradition as Bazin and Didi-Huberman who relate photography to the Shroud of Turin[12] as well as to the *acheiropoieta*, the images of Christ that were not manmade but emerged through pure contact with the face of Christ.[13] As Peter Geimer points out, these images share with photography-as-magic the understanding of the importance of their conditions of emergence and not of their indexical character. Or rather, the indexical character does not directly refer to the represented reality, but to the fragments of reality that are indirectly and accidentally present in the image — a blind spot

---

[9] Ibid., 8.

[10] See Georges Didi-Huberman, "La ressemblance par contact. Archéologie, anachronisme, et modernité de l'empreinte," in *L'impreinte* (Paris: Centre Georges Pompidou, 1997), 15–192.

[11] Roland Barthes, *Camera Lucida* (New York: Hill and Wang, 1982), 88.

[12] The linen cloth in which Jesus Christ was supposedly buried after his crucifixion and that bears the image of a man — Christ.

[13] See Peter Geimer, *Theorien der Fotografie. Zur Einführung* (Junius 2009), 65f.

of photographic production beyond the reach of the photographer's action.[14]

The condition of possibility for this blind spot is thus precisely photography's automatism, which channels the unintentional, a-subjective events and permits the unwanted, even unnoticed details to be present in the image. The disappearance of the author-subject through the automatic process is rephrased by Rudolf Arnheim in his "Photography — Being and Expression" from 1978 as the "uncanny" of photography: "What is uncanny about photography is that the picture comes into being the moment one presses, without previously having been involved in any way. The trigger on the little machine. Neither the hand nor the eye needs to do anything further."[15]

In a similar manner, Bazin writes that "only photography derives an advantage from his [man's] absence."[16] Arnheim admits that this absence of the will of the photographer represents an extreme, although relevant, case — but it is easily traced back to William Henry Fox Talbot's first definition of photography as

---

[14] Geimer recalls that the (more or less) contemporary discourse that relates photography and magic (as Benjamin, Susan Sontag, Roland Barthes and Jean Baudrillard among others do) borrows the vocabulary of William Henry Fox Talbot's first definition of photography as the magic of the cast in his *The Pencil of Nature* (1844-46). Whereas the intervention of the creating hand between the object and its copy in the image seems to make sense, the photographic production remains less transparent as it seems to happen by itself, only through the impression of light, without any human intervention (see Geimer, *Theorien...*,15f.).

[15] Rudolf Arnheim, "Die Fotografie — Sein und Aussage," in *Die Seele in der Silberschicht. Medi- entheoretische Texte. Photographie—Film—Rundfunk*, ed. Helmut H. Diederichs (Frankfurt: Suhrkamp, 2004), 6–42; on p. 38, quoted by Geimer, "Image as trace: Specu- lations about an Undead Paradigm," in *differences. A journal of Feminist Cultural Studies*, Vol. 18, N° 1, 2007, 7-28; above: 19.

[16] Bazin, "The Ontology...," 4-9, above, 7.

"the magic of the cast" in his *The Pencil of Nature* (1844–46).

> It frequently happens [...] and this is one of the charms of photography — that the operator himself discovers on examination, perhaps long afterwards, that he has depicted many things he had no notion of at the time. Sometimes inscriptions and dates are found upon the buildings, or printed placards most irrelevant, are discovered upon their walls: sometimes a distant dial-plate is seen, and upon it — unconsciously recorded — the hour of the day at which the view was taken.[17]

Such description resonates with Walter Benjamin's "optical unconscious," which he introduces in his "Little History of Photography" to describe the photographic technique and "its devices of slow motion and enlargement"[18] — devices that unveil fractions of reality that the photographer, when taking the picture, cannot perceive with his bare eye and only "unconsciously"

---

[17] William Henry Fox Talbot, "The Pencil of Nature," in *Henry Fox Talbot: Selected Texts and Bibliography*, ed. Mike Weaver (Boston: G. K. Hall, 1992), 75–103; above, 94; quoted by Geimer, "Image as trace...," 7-28; above, 19.

[18] Benjamin, "Little History of Photography," 511. A very similar formulation can be found in Benjamin's essay on the technical reproduction of art where he analyzes the destruction of the aura through technical reproduction and especially cinema in which context the reference to slow motion makes more sense. Benjamin sees an evolution from photography towards cinema, which is, as he explains, the most powerful agent of the masses. A filmic example of this optical unconscious can be found in Michelangelo Antonioni's *Blow Up* (1966), where the enlargement of a photograph leads to the discovery of a crime scene.

acknowledges. It is this essential unpredictability of photography that Benjamin calls "the tiny spark of contingency,"[19] and which Siegfried Kracauer refers to when he acknowledges the "accentuation of the accidental" as an elementary characteristic of photography.[20] It is also what Barthes's *punctum* refers to, since it occupies the image by accident, for purely contingent reasons and, despite this, becomes its most important hermeneutical element.

PHOTOGRAPHIC FICTION

Nevertheless, that the automatism of the camera inherently produces a moment of loss of control, and therefore comprises an aesthetic or creative element, is not something the viewer can sense at first in Douglas's highly constructed images. Rather s/he has to rely on the fictional superstructure that the artist provides in order to *illustrate* the double nature of photographic automatism: the images shown in *Entertainment* are from 1946-1951. The form of presentation of these images — chosen by Douglas and adopted in the exhibition — is that of a "chronicle," that is, of a linear unfolding of time. The aim of this strict, though fictional, chronology is to make palpable the dislocation in the understanding of the medium of photography itself. Douglas tells us, that the first contact of his fictitious photographer with

[19] Ibid., 510.

[20] Siegfried Kracauer, *Theory of Film* (Princeton: Princeton University Press, 1997). See especially the first chapter on photography, 3-26.

photographic technique, in 1945, is almost immediate due to the automatism inscribed in the technical apparatus — the photographer did not have any knowledge of photography, and the technique of photography is almost self-explanatory.[21] It is only gradually, that he comes to believe, "that photographers must employ fictional ruses if they are to create a convincing visual document of their era…the photographs of *Midcentury Studio* reflect their maker's dawning consciousness of the slippery nature of the medium that he employs."[22]

What Christopher Phillips suggests is that the gradual fictionalization of reality as the means to *better* represent reality derives from the gradual loss of

---

[21] As Christopher Phillips points out, the character of the fictitious photographer is inspired by several real-life photographers, among them the legendary Arthur Fellig known as Weegee; Bill Woods and his visual archive of the arrival of modern consumer culture in the American Southwest; and the Vancouver based photographer Raymond Munro, who, as Phillips tells us, "was a flamboyant figure who, following service as a fighter pilot in World War II, worked as an aviator, stunt parachutist, hypnotist, ambulance driver, muckraking journalist, and award-winning press photographer… Just after the war, Munro seems to have casually talked his way into a position as a photographer and journalist with the *Vancouver Sun*, confident that he could pick up the necessary skills on the job." Christopher Phillips, "The Adventure of a Photographer," in *Stan Douglas: Midcentury Studio*, ed. Tommy Simoens (Antwerp: Ludion, 2011), 11.

[22] Ibid. In his book, *The Politics of Aesthetics: The Distribution of the Sensible*, Jacques Rancière explains the shift from a representative to an aesthetic regime of the arts in almost exact the same terms only replacing the visual logic by the logic of thinking: "The real must be fictionalized in order to be thought." (Jacques Rancière, *The Politics of Aesthetics: The Distribution of the Sensible* (London: Continuum Books, 2004), 38. And he explains: "It is a matter of stating that the fiction of the aesthetic age defined models for connecting the presentation of facts and forms of intelligibility that blurred the border between the logic of facts and the logic of fictions." Rancière, *The Politics of…*," 38. The aesthetic revolution is hence concerned with these fictions: i.e., with "*material* rearrangements of signs and images, relationships between what is seen and what is said, between what is done and what can be done" Rancière, *The Politics of…*," 39. The boundary between documentary and fictional images is dissolved inasmuch as Rancière, reversing the Aristotelian hierarchy between historiography and tragedy, attributes the greater capacity of fictional invention to the documentary since it is not subjected to a "plot," a story, a narrative punch line. This dissolution also affects the status of the image in itself, and points at what Douglas via his fictitious photographer refers to as the "slippery nature" of the medium.

confidence in the photographic medium and its mimetic capacities, and this becomes apparent in the images in their ever more staged reality. While a first example, the white paint that deletes the person inside the suit in *Demobilization Suit, 1945* is still a rather crude intervention into the represented reality, the technique gets more sophisticated as the years go by. A more flagrant example of this fictionalization is palpable in the two images of the dancers, *Dancer I, 1950* and *Dancer II, 1950*, where the superimposition of images — that was also Dziga Vertov's preferred "trick" in his early films in order to distort the filmic reality — suggests a more subtle manipulation of the represented reality and refers to the animation of the images through film.[23]

Nevertheless the priority of *Entertainment* seems to lie less with the formal aspects of this fictionalization, as the exhibition explicitly addresses the "slippery nature" of photography under the auspices of "entertainment" that embraces games of chance, magic tricks, show business, sports games, or circus acts. While, following Phillips's hypothesis, the images' focus on the transfiguration of reality *in* the image, on the level of representation (and therefore continue the discussion about the subjective capacity of the photographic image), the selection presented here stresses the unsettling of reality *in reality*: that is through magic or gambling tricks, by highlighting

[23] Even though today superimposition might also seem a very restricted means of fictionalization, it is one that rests upon the technical skills of early and midcentury photography. In times of Photoshop, this cautious intervention into the image through superimposition might appear rather archaic, but it demonstrates that the discussion about the subjectivism of photography is not a discussion that only exists regarding digital photography. It not only addresses digital post-production of the images, but also analog techniques insofar as the choice of the cutout of reality represented, the angle, perspective, or exposure time are concerned.

the doubt or uncertainty of whether to believe in reality or not.

The selection of images "demonstrates" the fictional photographer's belief in the magic of photography by representing a magical intervention in reality within the larger field of entertainment. Therefore these images expose the fictionalization (or staging) of reality that photography necessarily undertakes — even when it is immediate or "accidental" — in a very specific way, by reconstructing or re-enacting the discourse around this magical realism itself as their "idiom." The images "speak" magic realism, but they themselves *are not* magic realism, but calculated studio photography. The invention of the midcentury photographer is thus Stan Douglas's own fictional ruse that allows him, through another fictional ruse (photography) to represent reality, but a reality that is in itself already an uncertain one — the unstable reality of the game of chance or of the magic trick.

PHOTOGRAPHIC ABSTRACTION

Stan Douglas's *Midcentury Studio* thus does not operate insomuch as a relocation of the discussion about photographic realism or photography-as-art, rather it takes the rearticulation of this discussion as the *status quo* of photography and as a departure point. It is the theoretical milieu his realistic images evolve in — it is the picture language they speak. The question of the aesthetic difference between reality and representation is relocated to diegetic reality itself, which appears as highly uncertain both in a historical dimension — the postwar years —

and in the singularity of the depicted activities such as gambling or juggling, for instance. This uncertainty of reality itself and its relation to the photographic image has been recently discussed by Hito Steyerl in terms of abstraction.[24] Steyerl rearticulates the discussion about the indexical character of the photographic image by pointing at the fact that today images become more and more "abstract," that is, digitally "blurred," "fuzzy," "pixelated;" for example, the photographs made by a CNN war-correspondent with a mobile telephone taken from inside a military vehicle in Iraq in 2003 and directly transmitted to US television. The euphoria the war correspondent feels because his images bring the reality of war in real time to American households is contrasted with the pictures themselves, which tell almost nothing: greenish surfaces like abstract compositions that have no similarity to any concrete reality. Nevertheless, these images are perceived as documentary images, as "authentic" testimonies, as evidence.

Steyerl argues that this paradox defines the basic principle of contemporary documentary images: doubt about the reality depicted by these images is their major feature. This doubt gives way to the substitution of the question of objectivity or reliability of the image by the desire for intensity — translated by the increasing importance of immersive artistic imagery. This "documentary feeling" replaces "documentary seeing/vision" and introduces the paradigm of affective identification into the alleged neutrality and critical distance of the documentary maker. Documentary images

[24] Hito Steyerl, *Die Farbe der Wahrheit* (Vienna: Thuria & Kant, 2008).

no longer *represent* a reality, but *express the doubt* about the uncertainty of their representative value, reflecting the doubt of a whole era, as Steyerl claims. The blurred greenish surfaces — that are due to the automatism of the cell phone cameras and their extreme mobility — are the expression of the uncertainty of their time. Hence "abstract documentarianism" is a question of form, not of content: reality is shaped into the form of the images — their blurriness — in a mimetic, necessary and unquestionable way. It is through their contextualization that the relation to a specific reality can be deduced. And it is therefore only by reconstructing the context — their conditions of emergence as Geimer has put it — by reintroducing the images into an archive of similar images and discourses that they unfold their significance: their abstraction challenges their (historical) contextualization.

This is therefore another, more contemporary but likewise technically-determined answer that can be given to the dilemma of automatic realism. The photographic image is no longer a "copy" of reality; rather, its indexical character retreats into the formal aspect of the image, an abstraction that reflects a state of things. To sum up, one could say that the history of photography consists of the refutation of automatic realism and claims either accidental details or abstraction as the negation of faith in authenticity. Either there is always something unexpected and unintentional in the image, or the photographic images have become abstract and are therefore in need of a critical contextualization. While the former seems to give way to a romanticization of photographic representation, the latter refers to a critical paradigm whose imperative is the accurate ethical manipulation of images and their context of origin as well as of exhibition.

A VISUAL BILDUNGSROMAN

But Douglas's *Midcentury Studio* images, and specifically the selection of *Entertainment* and their triple destabilization of reality, take things a step further and provide a meta-level where the *history* of photography becomes the *story* told by the images of a fictitious postwar photographer: the acknowledgement of the accidental character of photography as well as to an uncertainty paradigm, one that reflects the uncertainty of a historical moment and challenges an affective contextualization of the images. The images in *Midcentury Studio* presents us with a chronological history of photography that depicts the growing doubt in the naïve ontology of photography. Nevertheless this doubt does not affect the images (that would become either "accidental" or "abstract"). On the contrary, the images of *Midcentury Studio* strictly obey (and re-enact) the realistic imperative of studio photography and are meticulously constructed, i.e. they "construct" accidental moments and an atmosphere of uncertainty, instead of representing them, or rather they represent them by constructing them. The images that result from the fictitious practice of the fictitious photographer (whose *persona* Douglas adopts here), are therefore highly artificial; i.e., artificially produced magical — or accidental or uncertain — moments. This is the frame of Douglas's "story," of his visual *Bildungsroman* that addresses the instability of the postwar moment, the need for entertainment, games and amusement of the postwar population of a North American city, its normalization through distraction. The "story" — or the meta-narrative that Douglas constructs through but also in addition to the images — "represents" the main topics of the indexicality of photography: the belief in automatic realism, its refutation through the discovery of the creativity of photography's automatism, photography as magic, and photography as the reflection of an uncertain moment in time — without identifying with any of them.

Instead of adopting the hypothesis of photography as an accidental process, or that of an abstract documentarianism whose significance is produced by the analysis of the genealogical context of its production and features the desire for intensity, Stan Douglas's *Midcentury Studio* enacts the different refutations of a naturalistic photographic realism through an *artificial* naturalistic realism, which means through the representation of the representation of reality. *Midcentury Studio* does therefore not abide by the critical movement of unveiling a hidden truth in order to better understand its implications. It does not present a counter-truth or reintroduce an image into its context, either through an analysis in terms of the power-knowledge strategies that lie behind the production of images, or through the affective and emotional identification featured by the uncertainty of the blurred contemporary image itself. Nor does it believe in the significance of the one and only decisive moment that accidentally and automatically is captured within the image, and whose mechanism it exposes. On the contrary, through the accurate historical restaging of a precise postwar moment that is explicitly reflected within the images, Douglas re-enacts both the negation or suspension of the hypothesis of the documentary uncertainty derived from the uncertain state of things, as well as that of the reign of the uncanny detail inscribed in the photographic image, thereby artificially "recreating" — narrating — the indexical or realist hypothesis. While the contemporary uncertainty of reality, the doubt about its truth value, gives way to the blurriness of the documentary images whose "truth" relies on an affective identification through contextualization, the population of Douglas's acknowledged staged (or fake) documentary images of the midcentury reality react to its uncertainty in a different mode: Through an intensification of *reality* by "entertainment" that is meticulously even though fictitiously recounted, restaged and assembled in an archive of mid 1950s prototypes. Unlike the contemporary abstract documentary images, these portraits "represent" the uncertain historical and social conditions of the midcentury characters through extensive limpidity (that is not without recalling August Sander's physiognomic portraits of the early twentieth century), recreated in the fictitious midcentury studio (in the artificial milieu where everyday life of the 1950s is reanimated). Here, every detail is controlled and designed; everything is calculated, even flying daggers and oranges suspended in the air. Nothing is left to chance and nothing is uncertain or abstract. There are no "decisive moments," no magic, no authenticity or truth, only construction.

It is in this sense, that Douglas comes back to the insight of his fictitious character; i.e., the need for "fictional ruses" (or the need to fictionalize reality, as Jacques Rancière has put it) in order to "understand" reality. In his "Little History of Photography," Benjamin refers this paradox back to Bertolt Brecht's understanding of photography as a construction of an artificial situation within the logic of the alienation effect and contrasts it with its "creative" interpretation:

> But because the true face of this kind of photographic creativity is the advertisement or association, its logical counterpart is the act of unmasking or construction. As Brecht says: 'The situation is complicated by the fact that less than ever does the mere reflection of reality reveal anything about reality. A photograph of the Krupp works or the AEG tells us next to nothing about these institutions. Actual reality has slipped into the functional. The reification of human relations — the factory, say — means that they are no longer explicit. So something must in fact be built up, something artificial, posed.' We must credit the Surrealists with having trained the pioneers of such photographic construction.[25]

The tension between the hypothesis of the necessarily aleatory or accidental dimension of photography and its meticulous *mise en scène*, its "construction," is thus at the heart of *Midcentury Studio*, and its complete reversal of the documentary Weegee-esque strategy through its own

[25] Benjamin, "Little History of Photography," 526.

"photographic construction," which is not "Surrealist" in the way Benjamin refers to it, but consists of artificial re-enactments and reconstructions of the studio, the technical equipment, the décor. But it does not settle for this insight into the constructedness of reality and its representation (for which abstraction is only its *ultima ratio*); i.e., for the strategy that unveils that something apparently "accidental" or "magic" is de facto constructed or artificially produced. What Douglas's images ultimately point at is the disconnection that operates between the form of the image and its content — never does the accidental invade the frame other then as clearly marked as "accidental" (i.e., on the diegetic level) nor does the uncertainty of the 1950s postwar atmosphere affect the distinctness of the black-and-white photographs.

On the contrary — and this is where Stan Douglas's project is fully consequent with its premise and therefore differs from the mainstream "critical art" that features an analogy between form and content in order to deploy its criticalness — the aleatory and the uncertain, as the main hypothesis for his journey into the history of photography, always remain the *content* of the images, not their form, a content that is artificially staged — paradigmatically through suspended objects in the air — but whose accidental character does not affect the form of the image that is perfectly calculated. Douglas, through his fictitious photographer, constructs a history of photography around the aleatory as an aesthetic category that bundles the different stages of the photographic discussion. But he does not construct an aleatory history; rather his "history" takes the form of a "chronology." The "aleatoric event" is exposed as the *object*, while the form of the images obeys the strict rules of studio photography and finds itself in opposition to the immediacy of the 1950s photojournalism of Weegee and others that it re-enacts.

By exposing this tension between immediacy and technical mediatedness, between chance and utter calculation, between quick and mobile photojournalism and the ponderous studio techniques, and ultimately between form and content, Douglas's work relates the history of photography as a history of deconstruction that endlessly zigzags between the belief in photographic evidence and the discovery of its unsustainability, or between the assumption of a documentary image and its fictionalization. Nevertheless this discovery is not presented as the "new truth" of photography — it simply appears as another belief, another speculation about the essence of the photographic art, which, by essence, does not exist.

Clown, 1946, 2010
Digital silver print mounted
on Dibond aluminum
47 x 59”

Cricket Pitch, 1951, 2010
Digital silver print mounted
on Dibond aluminum
102 x 60”

Dancer II, 1950, 2010
Digital silver print mounted
on Dibond aluminum
72 x 59”

Flame, 1947, 2010
Digital silver print mounted
on Dibond aluminum
28 x 35”

Hockey Fight, 1951, 2010
Digital silver print mounted
on Dibond aluminum
98 x 60”

Juggler, 1946, 2010
Digital silver print mounted
on Dibond aluminum
58 x 83”

Passe-tête, 1946, 2010
Digital silver print mounted
on Dibond aluminum
47 x 59”

Rings, 1947, 2010
Digital silver print mounted
on Dibond aluminum
28 x 35”

Malabar People:
Bandleader, 1951, 2010
Digital silver print mounted
on Dibond aluminum
30 x 40”

Malabar People:
Bouncer, 1951, 2010
Digital Silver Print mounted
on Dibond Aluminium
30 x 40”

Malabar People:
Cab Driver, 1951, 2010
Digital silver print mounted
on Dibond aluminum
30 x 40”

Malabar People:
Construction Worker, 1951, 2010
Digital Silver Print mounted
on Dibond Aluminium
30 x 40”

Malabar People:
Dancer, 1951, 2010
Digital Silver Print mounted
on Dibond Aluminium
30 x 40”

Malabar People:
Female Impersonator, 1951, 2010
Digital silver print mounted
on Dibond aluminum
30 x 40”

Malabar People:
Logger, 1951, 2010
Digital silver print mounted
on Dibond aluminum
30 x 40” (outer dimensions)

Malabar People:
Longshoreman, 1951, 2010
Digital silver print mounted
on Dibond aluminum
30 x 40”

Malabar People:
Musician, 1951, 2010
Digital silver print mounted
on Dibond aluminum
30 x 40”

Malabar People:
Owner/Bartender, 1951, 2010
Digital Silver Print mounted
on Dibond Aluminium
30 x 40”

Malabar People:
Single Woman I, 1951, 2010
Digital silver print mounted
on Dibond aluminum
30 x 40”

Malabar People:
Single Woman II, 1951, 2010
Digital silver print mounted
on Dibond aluminum
30 x 40”

Malabar People:
Student, 1951, 2010
Digital Silver Print mounted
on Dibond Aluminium
30 x 40”

Malabar People:
Waitress I, 1951, 2010
Digital silver print mounted
on Dibond aluminum
30 x 40”

Malabar People:
Waitress II, 1951, 2010
Digital silver print mounted
on Dibond aluminum
30 x 40”

Malabar People:
West-Side Lady, 1951, 2010
Digital silver print mounted
on Dibond aluminum
30 x 40”

All works courtesy the artist and David Zwirner, New York except *Clown, 1946*, 2010 which is from the Hort Family Collection.

Stan Douglas has had numerous exhibitions at prominent institutions worldwide. Recent solo exhibitions have taken place at Staatsgalerie Stuttgart and Württembergischer Kunstverein, Stuttgart (2007); Studio Museum, Harlem, New York (2005); kestnergesellschaft, Hanover (2003); Serpentine Gallery, London (2002); and Vancouver Art Gallery/The Power Plant (1999). His work has been included in recent group exhibitions at the 4th Moscow Biennale (2011); Guggenheim Museum, New York (2010); ZKM/Museum für Neue Kunst, Karlsruhe (2010); 3rd ICP Triennial of Photography and Video, New York (2009); Hirshhorn Museum and Sculpture Garden, Washington, DC (2008): Centre Pompidou, Paris (2007); 51st Venice Biennale (2005); 25th São Paulo Biennale (2002); and documenta X (1997). He lives and works in Vancouver. His work is represented by David Zwirner, New York.

Louis Kaplan is Professor of History and Theory of Photography and New Media in the Graduate Department of Art of the University of Toronto and Chair of the Department of Visual Studies at the Mississauga campus. He is the author of *American Exposures: Photography and Community in the Twentieth Century* (Minnesota, 2005) and he is currently working on a book dealing with the topic of *Photography and Humor* to be published by Reaktion Books (London). Kaplan serves as senior research consultant to the Shpilman Institute for Photography in Tel Aviv, Israel.

Maria Muhle is Academic Assistant at the Institute for Media Studies, Bauhaus-University Weimar. Her research focuses on contemporary political and aesthetical theory, and especially on the notions of "aesthetic realism," documentarianism, and on strategies of re-enactment in the context of a political aesthetics. She is the co-founder of August Verlag Berlin, a publishing house for theory at the crossroads of philosophy, politics and arts.

Melanie O'Brian is Curator & Head of Programs at The Power Plant. She has curated exhibitions nationally and internationally, including a program of offsite projects at Artspeak (2008-2010) where she was formerly Director/Curator. She is the editor of *Vancouver Art & Economies* (Arsenal Pulp Press/Artspeak, 2007) and *Judgment and Contemporary Art Criticism* (Artspeak/Fillip, 2010), and has contributed to catalogues and magazines such as C, Mix, Fillip, X-Tra, and Yishu.

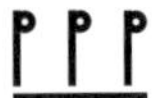

ISBN: 978-1-894212-34-2

Library and Archives Canada Cataloguing in Publication

Kaplan, Louis, 1960-
Stan Douglas : Entertainment / edited by Melanie O'Brian ; contributions by Louis Kaplan, Maria Muhle.

(Power Plant Pages)
Includes bibliographical references.
Catalogue of an exhibition held at The Power Plant,
Toronto, ON. in the winter 2011-2012.
ISBN 978-1-894212-34-2

1. Douglas, Stan--Exhibitions. I. Douglas, Stan II. O'Brian, Melanie, 1973- III. Muhle, Maria, 1976- IV. Power Plant (Art gallery) V. Title. VI. Series: Power Plant Pages

N6549.D68A4 2011 709.2
C2011-907071-5

Published in conjunction with the exhibition *Stan Douglas: Entertainment: Selections from Midcentury Studio*

The Power Plant

10 December 2011 – 4 March 2012

Curated by Melanie O'Brian

The Power Plant
231 Queens Quay West
Toronto, ON M5J 2G8 Canada

Editor: Melanie O'Brian
Design: Sameer Farooq, New Ink
Coordination: Edward Kanerva
Copy editing: Rosemary Heather, Jon Davies
Printing and binding: Shapco Printing, Inc., Minneapolis, MN

Acting Director's Acknowledgements

This succinct publication is the first in a series of scholarly readers entitled *Power Plant Pages*. It also accompanies the exquisite exhibition *Stan Douglas: Entertainment: Selections from Midcentury Studio*. The Power Plant sincerely thanks Stan Douglas for his generosity, intelligence, and rigor, enabling a thoughtful and engaging presentation of work. Acknowledging a 1999 exhibition of Douglas's work at The Power Plant, this exhibition marks a revised engagement of ideas between the artist and curator Melanie O'Brian.

The Power Plant acknowledges the generous support of the Presenting Sponsor of the exhibition, Rogers Communications. We would also like to thank the assistance and support of David Zwirner, New York; The Hort Family Collection; the staff at Stan Douglas Studio, particularly Linda Chinfen; writers for the publication Louis Kaplan and Maria Muhle; and countless others who supported the realization of this project. Finally, The Power Plant benefits from the significant ongoing support of the Canada Council for the Arts, Harbourfront Centre, the Ontario Arts Council and the Toronto Arts Council.

Christy Thompson, Acting Director

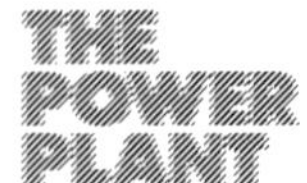

MAJOR SUPPORTERS

Canada Council for the Arts

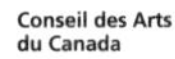

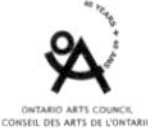

torontdartsbouncil
An arm's length body of the City of Toronto

Harbourfront centre

PRESENTING SPONSOR

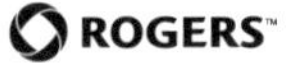